I GIVE THE DUMB KIDS HOPE

57 LIFE LESSONS TO TAKE YOU FROM A LIFE OF DESPAIR TO MULTI-MILLIONAIRE

I GIVE THE DUMB KIDS HOPE

*57 LIFE LESSONS TO TAKE
YOU FROM A LIFE OF DESPAIR
TO MULTI-MILLIONAIRE*

BY BRIAN WILL

DEDICATION

This book is dedicated first to my children, who it was ultimately written for; my daughter Stephanie and my son Michael. I could not have asked for better children. They are the light of my life, and I can't imagine not being a part of their lives. As I like to say to them, "I love you more than chocolate chip cookies...and I SERIOUSLY love chocolate chip cookies!!!"

It is also dedicated to everyone who read the first three to four chapters and encouraged me to finish it, as well as my beta readers who have given me so much incredible input into the final version. Anita, Stephanie, Michael, Don, Bill, and my editor Hilary... Thank you so much for helping me get this one done. It means a lot to me.

TABLE OF CONTENTS

TABLE OF CONTENTS

FOREWORD

When Brian asked me to write his foreword, we both paused and had to ask, "Can the editor write the foreword? Is that allowed?" But then, in true Brian fashion, he declared that it didn't matter if we were breaking the rules.

It's fitting.

I was immensely flattered.

In the short time I have known Brian, I have been impressed with his attitude. And I don't just mean that the man is steeped in positivity, although he definitely is. I mean, Brian appears to be made out of the same material as a fishing bobber. It doesn't matter what circumstances try to hold him down. He pops right back to the top!

When it comes to overcoming, Brian is a veteran.

Let me explain...

Sometimes we wonder why we are alive, and this question might seem heavier and as if it doesn't even matter when we are born behind the eight ball as Brian was. I think Brian is here to prove to people that the beauty of life is created by us. That we hold the capacity to make miracles. That circumstances are not eternal reality. That at any time, when you are unhappy, you can manufacture your own happiness. All it takes is a little innovative thinking. I know after reading his book, that's one of the reasons that Brian is here.

To spread that word.

Everything in Brian's world moves. If he doesn't like where he is, he isn't afraid to crumple up his plans and start over. We can all learn from that. So often, we seek security in standing still. I know I am guilty of that.

And that is exactly why his story needs to be told.

He was put on this earth to tell it, even though living it was, at times, excruciating.

That didn't matter to him. Moving ahead did.

Brian refused to stagnate. He has run the gamut of life and is still going. And I am not just talking about globe-trotting. He makes his life what he wants it and is on a mission to understand every fragile part of it. To dive more deeply into understanding himself and others. It's a gift to be curious about what the whole of you contains, and it is a gift to know your own power as you refuse to be a prisoner. Yet it's a greater gift to share that power with the rest of the world.

How often have you found yourself to be the person holding you back? *I Give the Dumb Kids Hope* brings you face to face with a person who has been through it all—and who recognized he didn't want to hold himself back anymore. This realization actually hit when he was just a kid. In Brian's eyes, it wasn't worth it to live an existence that was less than what he dreamt of. It didn't matter who didn't believe in him. He wouldn't be stopped.

Brian shares the details of his trying childhood that will make you cry, his desperate grasping for the love of his kids and wife without knowing what it meant to really love. He spins poverty tales that will make you chuckle and shake your head and confides that he suffered a rare disassociation born of tremendous and repeated trauma. Then there is his latest life chapter where he dominated four industries and made millions—with barely a diploma and a few college classes under his belt. Yet, he is still standing—purely under his own resilience.

And Brian is a deft and naturally descriptive storyteller. He is of the ilk of authors who don't hold back. He isn't shy about telling you of his mistakes, about how he sought to be "ambitiously lazy"—a term that when I first heard him say it made me burst out laughing. But he's clever like that. Taking stock of potential and the best way to reach it.

Speaking of laughing out loud, you will not want to miss the chapter on his special financial strategy called "McDonald's Safety Net." I promise you won't regret it!

You are about to learn that obstacles don't mean anything to Brian. He leaps over them without knowing where he will land, and if you ever wanted to know a man who goes all-in, it's him.

When Brian and I first talked about working together, and he told me about everything he had overcome in his life and what he has achieved, I was so excited for him to share his message because, as he talked, I knew that he would help others.

We all need people who show us that fear is just a tiny monster we have enlarged in our minds. We need to know we can shrink that monster and discover that our dreams are livable —in fact, they are critical to becoming our very best selves. To finding elusive happiness.

As Brian jokes about giving the dumb kids hope, he has forgotten one key element: he is not dumb, or maybe as the old saying goes: he is as "dumb as a fox."

I think he was misunderstood and taken for granted and then went on to discover that he has some pretty great ideas and that he loves one thing more than anything else: being a father. He learned that he is the one who had to give himself a shot. Because he was the only one who could and the only one who mattered. Just like your belief in yourself is the only thing that matters.

Soak up his stories and use their lessons to put your life on your most desired trajectory. And hey, if you want to skip ahead to the life lessons' section, you can find it at the back of the book. But we both hope you will first consume the pages Brian has written just for you.

In the end, you will have no choice but to let *I Give the Dumb Kids Hope* give you hope.

It just happens.

Enjoy the ride…and the read.

~Hilary Jastram

J. Hill Marketing/Bookmark Editing House

PREFACE

Years ago, my children attended a private school from elementary to graduation. This particular private school, much like all of them, I assume, was very big on college prep. The kids would go to school all day, and at night, they would come home and still have three hours of homework.

My daughter would be up most nights until two in the morning studying. Many nights I would see her sitting on the kitchen floor with a notebook. She would usually have a candle lit beside her on the floor, as well. I asked her one night why she was sitting on the floor with a candle, and she told me she had to be uncomfortable to study, or she would fall asleep.... and "Why the candle?" I asked... "Because I like the smell," she said.

I would routinely come into the kitchen at night after waking up and find her there in the middle of the floor. This would turn into semi arguments with my daughter about her needing to go to bed and get some sleep. She would tell me the same thing every time... "I need to study." The pressure from school was intense. She needed to get good grades, so she could get into a good school, so she could get a good job. That is what the school preached to these kids during their entire high school career. They needed to be **smart**.

I am not against any of those principles... I like having smart kids... I believe in studying hard...getting good grades...getting into a good school, and getting a good job. However, I do believe there is a balance, and the school was pushing these kids too hard. When I told my daughter to go to bed, she would get mad and tell me I wasn't supporting her educational goals and that she needed good grades... I would fire back... "Then how do you explain me?"

I barely graduated high school. I think my grade point average was around 1.2. I was almost held back my junior year because I had missed forty-two out of around ninety days of class and skipped the midterms. I later got into Ohio State but then dropped out of college after a year.

Despite my checkered scholastic past, we were living in a giant house that my daughter's friends and teachers referred to as the castle. I was a multi-millionaire and didn't have to go to work. So, I wanted to know: "If education is so important... How do you explain me?!"

One night, as we were having this argument again, I asked the question once more..."How do you explain me?!" Her answer was... "You know, Daddy, me and my friends were just talking about you the other day. We came to the conclusion that **you give the dumb kids hope!!!**" Now by "dumb," she meant kids who got Bs and Cs in private school. Even with my very limited educational background, I gave them hope!

I have to tell you I am very proud of that statement.

This book is about some of the life lessons I have tried to teach my children over the last twenty-five years. These are the type of lessons that they don't teach you in any school. They are learned the hard way, from trial and error. They come from failure...success...failure...failure...and success. The lessons are not so much for my children to use, but rather for them to learn from as adults. Hopefully, if they learn them, they can then teach them to their kids.

I believe that it is our job as parents to bring our kids up better than we were brought up. It is our responsibility to move them forward in the evolutionary chain of life so that future generations will be smarter and better equipped to handle the ups and downs and the things life throws at them.

At least that is my belief. My hope is also that you, the reader, will be able to learn some things through my experiences that you can apply to your life. The other option is that maybe you can give the book to your kids to help them learn some of those things you have been trying to teach them that they won't listen to you about. Since we all know our kids barely listen to our advice, maybe this will be a good third-party book about things they might need to hear.

What follows in these pages you are about to read are some of those experiences and lessons I want to pass on....that give the "dumb" kids hope.

INTRODUCTION

This book was originally intended as a book for my children about their dad. My goal was to get some of my stories down on paper, so they would have something tangible to remember me by when I'm gone.

I had talked about writing this book for over ten years but just couldn't get the motivation to sit down and actually do it. I think my ADHD was just too hard to overcome. My life is a constant barrage of information and thoughts and ideas that keeps me from just settling down for long tasks. I guess I am basically not built that way.

For my 50th birthday, I planned a trip to Key West. I didn't have a companion when I booked it; I figured I would find some-one before I left that would want to come with me. Unfortunately, or fortunately, I didn't find anyone and ended up going by myself.

Once there, I had a beautiful corner suite on the water with a gorgeous view...and nothing to do. After checking into my room, I was sitting on the porch wondering what to do to kill time. I picked up my iPad and turned it on, and there was the empty file with the book title on it, staring at me. It had been there for years. Since I was bored, I decided to start the book.

Not being a good typist, I began by dictating my thoughts into the word document. Once I started, I couldn't stop. I sat there the first day for around twelve hours dictating and then manu-ally correcting the autocorrect mistakes. I honestly didn't want to go to bed that night; I was on a roll and didn't want to lose the train of thought. The next day was the same; I spent another twelve hours dictating and correcting... I did the same thing the third day.

By the end of the third day, I had 24,000 words on paper. The book was half done. I decided that when I got home, I would finish the book pretty quickly. So, I left Key West and headed back to Atlanta. When I got home, I tried to pick the writing back up. For years, I tried to pick it back up, but every time I tried, I got distracted and stopped. The half-written book sat in the same file on my desktop for another five years.

Over the years, people would occasionally ask me about the book, and I would tell them it was half done. Several friends asked me if they could get a sneak peek. Not wanting to give a half-written rough draft out, I decided to let them see the first three or four chapters. After reading the beginning of the book, they all told me the same thing: I should actually write the book not just for my children, but for other people who might want, or need, to hear my story.

In February of 2020, I was headed out to Park City for a month of skiing. Another friend had asked to read the first couple chapters of the book, and after reading it, he told me I should finish it and get it out. For whatever reason, that motivated me. As I sat out in Park City, I would ski during the day and write more in the book at night. I ended up finishing the first rough draft while I was out there, and then I hired an editor to help me get it published.

It has been an interesting experience, and I have learned a lot about this process along the way. The actual writing time on this book is probably around fifteen days...over the last five years. In the truest fashion of the history of this book, I am now writing this introduction as I sit on the balcony of a house we rented for a week in St. John overlooking the ocean.

I guess I write the best when I am on vacation...somewhere other than home.

Brian

CHAPTER 1

NOW AND THEN

"Start where you are. Use what you have.
Do what you can." ~Arthur Ashe

"Everyone has their own journey...
This one is mine."

In the last twenty-five years, I have founded or co-founded six different, very successful companies in four different industries. I franchised a landscaping company, launched three start-ups in the insurance industry, as well as an internet marketing company, and I now own a chain of restaurants. I also founded many other companies that weren't successful at all, and that lost me a significant amount of money. This book is about both the winners and the losers, and the lessons I have learned about life along the way...but let's start with when everything went right....well, almost everything.

At their peak, five of my companies were worth hundreds of millions of dollars. Most of them became much more successful after I sold them. In short, I built them, and someone else took them to the next level. Three companies were sold to venture capital and private equity groups, and out of those three, one of those went public.

I have also consulted for multiple companies, from small businesses to multi-billion dollar private and public companies in the areas of sales and management. Today I own a very successful chain of restaurants in the Atlanta area. Now, I can't cook. I don't know how to bartend. I don't even know how to put an order into the POS (Point of Sale) ordering system. I never work in any of the locations, and except for the one by my house, I rarely ever go to any of them. There is at least one location that I have not stepped foot in in over a year. Still, I own these restaurants outright with no partners and no debt—and I call this my fourth career.

Over the past ten years and after finding some success in business, I also became a pilot and a divemaster. These are two of my favorite things in the world to do. I have walked around nine miles over two days on the Great Wall of China with my daughter. We didn't just walk the nice part you see in the movies; we were on the actual old broken, crumbling parts of the original wall. I ran with the bulls in Spain with both of my children. Yes, they ran with me, and yes, it was scary!! I have climbed four of the 14ers in Colorado. While in Tokyo, I climbed Mount Fuji with both my children. We got lost coming down the mountain and were the last three people to get on the last bus out. We were very close to spending the night alone on the mountain. That was a long and tough day. I swam from Alcatraz Island to San

Francisco during one of the annual Sharkfest swimming events, along with 800 other crazy people. I will never do that again! While in London, not only did I get to be one of the first people to tour the underground bunkers where Churchill led the war effort for Great Britain, I also had dinner that night in the same bunker with one of his daughters. The next night we had the privilege of having dinner in Winston Churchill's private home. It's basically a castle. The Queen's guards' marching band was out in full uniform, playing music as we arrived in a fleet of Mercedes Benz cars in the courtyard. We absolutely felt like royalty. Upon getting out of the car, they escorted us up the stairs to the front door where two guardsmen with trumpets played to announce us, and another made a formal announcement of who we were. The crowd applauded as we walked in—it was stuff straight out of the movies!

While in Italy, a small group of us were serenaded by The Three Tenors at a private dinner on Lake Como—located right next to a famous actor's house you've probably heard of. I have seen the actual painting of the Last Supper. Here is a little-known fact. I thought the painting of the last supper was in Paris in The Louvre. It's not!! It is actually a mural painted on the dining hall wall in a building in Milan, Italy. A door goes through the middle of it! During the war, when Milan was being bombed, all the buildings around this location were hit except this building that still stands today.

On another trip, my daughter and I toured the wine country in Stellenbosch, South Africa, by helicopter. I also took my daughter cage diving with great white sharks while there. I have dined inside the Eiffel Tower twice. I have been island hopping through the Virgin Islands on a private catamaran. I have sat on a private balcony and watched the annual jet boat races in Florida. I climbed The O2 in London. I have toured 3,000-year-old castles in Scotland and Ireland. I spend a month each winter in Park City, Utah skiing and four months a year at my beach place in Clearwater Beach, Florida. There are so many more adventures I've had in my life, and most of those I have experienced with both of my children. I have traveled the world, raised two amazing kids, and finally... For whatever reason, you are now reading my book.

"Now, let's put everything that I just shared in perspective."

As I said earlier, I graduated high school in 1983 with a 1.2-grade point average—having technically failed my junior year because I decided for whatever reason to skip my midterms. The truth is, I just didn't feel like going. Here is a tip: schools don't like that. We will get to this story later. Let's just say I was not a good student.

I tried going to college after a brief stint of active duty with the Ohio Air National Guard, but I couldn't do it and dropped out. I never learned to study in high school and was no better in college. I will tell that story later as well but let me share that it was more about anger and rebellion than anything else.

I moved to Atlanta, Georgia, for the first time in 1985 and got a job as a construction laborer hanging vinyl siding. I got fired.

Then I got a job as an assistant manager at a Little Caesars Pizza. I got fired. Next, I got a job as a waiter at a restaurant called Brick Works. I got fired from that job as well. I finally found my calling as a busboy at an Applebee's restaurant in 1985 and worked there until 1986.

Being a busboy was something I could be good at. I tell you all this because sometimes the way we start out in life doesn't mean we have to end up that way.

I certainly didn't start out with a bang. You would not have looked at me and thought, *wow, this guy is going somewhere.* Chances are, you would have looked and me and thought, *wow, this guy has NO future!*

Life Lesson...

Don't judge people's future by what you see today. Lots of great people started at the bottom and worked their way up...and lots of people at the top...have worked their way down.

In 1987, I moved back to Ohio and got married at the age of twenty-one. My new wife and I then moved in with my grandmother because I did not have a job, a car, or a place to live. I was not an example of the type of man I would want my daughter to marry. Newly married and after the honeymoon, I took a job as a laborer on a lawn maintenance crew, making four dollars an hour cutting grass. To this day, I'm not sure why my wife married me. She must have been crazy!

I have no education. I've been unemployed. I've worked crappy jobs. I've had no money. I've had no furniture. I've had to sell my furniture for money to eat after my first business failed, and I was broke with no income. When my mother came to my house and found out we had sold our furniture, she bought me more furniture. After she left, we sold the new furniture. I pawned my new wife's jewelry so we could feed the baby. I've been in jail. I've been fired more times than most people. At times I couldn't support my family. My children have had serious health issues. My daughter had open-heart surgery at the age of four, as well as she has a cataract that makes her legally blind in one eye. I've had my cars repossessed, and my utilities turned off. I've lost everything multiple times. I've had horrible credit. The banks would not let me open an account because I had too many bounced checks. I've had to pay my bills with money orders. I've gone hungry. I've had creditors blowing up my telephone, trying to collect money I didn't have. I've been under massive stress both from the world and from myself. I came from an extremely abusive home. I was kicked out at eighteen. I once considered selling my organs for money. (totally not kidding) I've been depressed and on medication for that, as well as have been pre-scribed sleeping pills because I could not go to sleep. My parents let me down. My father hid his existence from me for fifty years, and when I found him, he continued to lie to me and then denied I was his son for another five years. My mother lied about my father until I forced the information from her. My point is that I have been there and done that. If anybody understands starting from zero and having the deck stacked against you... I get it.

Sometimes I think back on all the events in my life and wonder if they happened for a reason. Was it an intentional act of God, fate, or karma that put me on this journey? Did this happen for a specific purpose? ...Maybe so I could relate to other people for some reason I don't know about... Maybe to be used in this book?? I often wonder, *why me?* Or did these random events have no meaning? Was it nothing more than good or bad luck that my life ended up on this path? These are questions I will never know the answer to...

So, how does the kid who barely graduated high school, who dropped out of college, and who could only keep jobs as a busboy and a lawn maintenance laborer go on to co-found $1 billion worth of companies and make millions of dollars and travel the world in the process?

Keep reading.

CHAPTER 2

MY PERSONAL DEMON

"I can't drown my demons. They know how to swim."
~From the song, "Can You Feel My Heart?"

I grew up a redheaded, bastard stepchild from a middle-class family in a small town in Ohio.

I do not use those terms lightly or in jest. I really do have red hair. I was a stepchild to an abusive stepfather, and I did not find out who my real father was until I was forty-five years old. It turns out I was the product of an affair while my mother was married. Growing up, I lived about ten miles from my bio-father and his family, which included a brother and sister I also didn't know about. During my senior year of high school, I even dated one of my sister's friends. Do you think our parents would have said something if I had dated my own sister?!?

The guy I thought was my father ignored me. I rarely saw him as he had three other sons with his new wife. He had divorced my mother when I was one year old. He knew the whole time that

I was not his son. Looking back, it makes sense that I was a second thought to him. He also was and is and still is an alcoholic.

I met my actual father two years ago. It took him five years after I initially found out who he was to admit I was his son. I also found out that he had two kids other than me. That brought his total to three, until last year, when one more popped up after taking a genetic test through 23andMe. So the current count is four, although we are waiting on more to pop up any day. Bio-dad was a player in the free love sixties.

I like to joke now that I have three ex-half-brothers, one ex-stepbrother, two ex-stepsisters, and now an actual half-sister and two half-brothers—one I have never met and one I only met this year. Same father different mothers. Are you confused yet?!

I grew up living with a stepfather. He is my only memory of a man in my life growing up. He was the head of our church other than the minister, and made us go to services every Sunday. So, he considered himself a good Christian man. He was also the Grand Master of the local masonic lodge. On the surface, he seemed like a good guy...however...

My stepfather liked to hit...mostly me, and probably my mother. He was physically, sexually, and emotionally abusive. During my entire childhood, I remember being terrified of being alone with him. I lived in fear every day of my life as a child. From the earliest age that I can remember, from about six until sixteen, I always knew that every time my mother would leave the house, I was going to get it. Then there were the threats that if I told anyone, it would be worse. So, I never said anything. Instead, I would watch my mother leave and get scared.

"My entire childhood, I was constantly told that I was worthless and would never amount to anything."

My stepfathers' other children would come over, and they were treated like normal kids. I was not. I remember as a teenager being told that I should probably learn how to drive a truck because I was so stupid that truck driving was probably the only thing I would be able to do as an adult. I can remember the conversation… I can remember where I was standing…what I was wearing, and what I was doing. There are so many memories burned into my head—like movies of my past that never go away. They still haunt me. This abuse went on for years and years. I will not get into details here, but I would never want any child to have to endure what I did. Today my stepfather would have gone to prison if anyone had found out what he was doing to me.

The hitting finally stopped when I was around sixteen. This was when I decided to start hitting back. The scene still plays in my head like it happened yesterday; it never goes away. We were out in the back of our property, cutting wood for the fireplace that winter. It was cold, and I was miserable. I don't remember the conversation exactly—except the part where my stepfather told me I was a useless piece of shit. "Useless as tits on a bore hog" was his favorite saying for me. I was told again that I was worthless and would never amount to anything. I remember hearing this at the age of sixteen and how it devastated me. He was the adult in my life who was supposed to be my protector. He was supposed to be the one I looked up to. I remember the emotion inside me welling up... Just writing this, I can still feel it today.

I started to cry and yelled and cursed at him. I told him I hated him. He told me again, "You are a stupid fucking 16-year-old," and then punched me in the face so hard he knocked me down. I hated him. I told him, "I will never be like you in any way, and if you ever hit me again, I will kill you."

I was done being hit. My stepfather was and always will be the demon in my life. I haven't seen him in thirty years other than pictures of him at church on Facebook. I assume he is still active there and pretends to be a godly man.

Life lesson...

Physical abuse is bad...but so is mental abuse. The words you say to people are incredibly powerful. Words can stay with you for life. Children especially will take your words as the absolute gospel and create their life around how you think of them. You can make a comment to someone, and it has the power to affect their life forever. So watch what you say. And if you realize you said something wrong, take it back immediately before it's too late.

CHAPTER 3

STARTING LIFE AT ZERO

"We all start at zero. We all start at the beginning.
Do not give up." ~Nick Vujicic

I was a mess as a child, teenager, and even as a young adult.

I had no direction, no real parents, and no idea how to be a human being. There were no examples in my life of how to be a functioning person. When I was around fourteen, my stepfather kept a loaded gun in a shoebox in my parents' closet. It was the kind with six bullets in the chamber. I can remember going in there many times to get the gun when he and my mom were not home. Sometimes I would just play with it. Sometimes, however, I put that gun to my head and thought about pulling the trigger. At least the pain and fear would stop. Something always stopped me. Maybe I was scared, or maybe it was something else. But I would always put the gun back and walk away. Those memories are as vivid as if I were still there today in the closet. I can feel that gun in my hand as I write this. The memory of it never goes away.

I was also angry with my mother as I grew up. Not just because of her treatment of me, but because she allowed my stepfather to do what he did.

My mother liked to slap me in the face when she was angry. I remember watching her brother and sisters slap their children around when we would visit Mississippi. They used either a hand or a flyswatter. I assume that is the way she and her siblings were raised, and it was natural for her to continue that pattern of abuse. Her abuse also stopped when I was sixteen when she came into my room one night.

We got into an argument. I was standing in the middle of my room, facing her. I can see it now in my mind: she was in a night-gown and a white robe. She brought her arm up and took a swing at me, and for the first time in my life, I blocked it. I didn't allow her to hit me. She looked at me with this shocked "I can't believe he didn't let me slap him" expression. Through my tears, I told her that was the last time she would ever hit me. If she tried it again, I was going to hit her back. She never hit me again. My relationship with my mother was destroyed as a child. She lost her parental authority over me and would never get it back. I'm talking about the kind of authority where you listen when your mother talks. The kind where you ask her for advice because she is supposed to be smarter and wiser than you. If you think about the way you are supposed to think about your mother, that was gone with me. I can't even imagine doing what was done to me, to my kids. It's too scary to even think about.

To this day, I do not know if she knew about the abuse from my stepfather…or if she didn't. I assume he was physically abusive to her as well. I do know he threatened to make me disappear if she ever left him. I also know that as a child and young adult, I didn't care if she knew or not. In my mind, I thought that *she should have known. She was my mother. She was supposed to protect me.* I would often think to myself, *how can she let these things happen...*and *why doesn't she love me?*

I was angry at her for everything that had happened, and I carried the majority of that anger toward her until I was about forty-five years old; when after a couple of years of counseling, I finally sat down with her for about four hours and let it out.

"The anger is still there, but at least today, I don't let it control me the way it used to. I recognize it for what it is and manage it."

When I graduated high school, my stepfather told me to leave and that I was not welcome in our home. I remember him saying, "This is my home, and you need to leave." So I left...rebellious, full of hate, with authority problems and a giant chip on my shoulder. Having no place to go and no shot at college, I joined the military. I laugh now thinking about this. I was so defiant and hated being told what to do, so of course, I joined the military.

Side notes...

I do remember thinking at that age that if I ever got married, I would never get divorced. The whole divorce and stepfather image in my head was so negative and so strong, divorce was just not something

19

I would ever do. Unfortunately, that plan didn't work out, and I would eventually get divorced.

I also knew that I would never touch my children. I could not even bring myself to spank them when they were growing up. I was absolutely terrified of what would happen if I laid a hand on either of them. I wasn't as much afraid of what would happen to them, as much as what would happen to me. Maybe it's like a recovering alcoholic taking another drink. I was afraid of the demon inside me coming out. So I never did raise a hand to them, not even once. And the funny thing is they turned out to be great kids. I know a lot of people think it's fine to use this sort of discipline, and some think it's necessary. I didn't. I don't. And I hope my children don't ever as well. Why in the world does anyone think a grown adult needs to hit a child? It makes me angry when I see this sort of abuse. Really angry...

My experience has shown me that people who grew up in the type of atmosphere I did tend to go one of three ways in life.

The first group allows their hurt and anger to turn them into the same type of people who abused them. They become abusers. My mother is an example of this, and I assume my stepfather is as well. They, in turn, pass that same abuse down to the next generation and the next generation after that. Many times they end up in trouble with the law. That cycle continues until someone chooses to break it. **The sins of the father...**

The second group becomes so mentally devastated that they do nothing with their life and struggle to ever move past their abuse. They don't find happiness or success of any kind, but meander through life struggling to survive. They are unhappy and blame the world for all their problems.

The third group takes that hate and anger and uses it. Often, they create tremendous success in life. We see them as actors, musicians, and businesspeople. Their hurt and anger become their single greatest ally in whatever avenue they pursue.

I fit in that third category, and I don't know why. Maybe its genetics, God, or something else, but for some reason, I didn't let my abuse completely destroy me. That anger, hate, and rage drove me in two specific directions in life. The first was never to live like or be like my stepfather. The second was to prove to him and the world that I was not the loser they thought I was. I was on a mission. I wanted to succeed. I wanted to be rich. I wanted to have the things I saw on TV and in magazines that I hated I didn't have. I was not just a truck driver. I wanted to win the game of life. More importantly, I needed to win the game of life so other people wouldn't look down on me. **I had to win...at any cost.**

I also wanted to get away.

"Something inside me told me that I had to leave...to escape... I had to remove myself from my family's influence and break the cycle."

I didn't have a real understanding of what it was I was doing at the time, or why it was so important that I leave. I figured that out much later as I reflected on my journey. But I had to cut off my family and everything I knew and start over. That was my job as an adult. To get my head straight and protect my future kids and family from that past and that sort of life. While I would be forced to deal with what had happened to me for the rest of my life, I would not allow my future children to be exposed to it. So I left. I didn't speak to my family for years. That was the right decision for me.

I hated my stepfather with every fiber of my being. I was angry and determined not to forgive or forget. But here's the funny thing about psychology and families (and I did not understand this until much later in life), by allowing that hate and anger to exist, I was allowing the person that I hated to continue to control my life twenty years after I removed my stepfather from it physically. He continued to influence everything I did. He influenced the decisions I made and the way that I treated my wife and children. That anger cost me my marriage. As long as I held onto that anger, he was as close to me as ever. The one person I so desperately wanted to get away from was with me twenty-four hours a day. He was in my head, taunting me.

Even today, as I have settled a lot of my issues in my life, the damage that has been done is still there. It's made me less of a father than I would have liked to have been. The part that is hard to accept is that you know what you did wrong, but you can't go back and fix it. That is the tough part, and the part I hope some of this book will help my children see and use to become even better parents than I was to them.

And here is the lesson.

You have to let go. If somebody does you wrong, you have to let go. If they hurt you or abuse you, you have to let it go. If you truly want that situation in your life to be gone, as hard as it is, and as much as you don't want to, you have to let it go and move on. Otherwise, the very thing that you hate will stay with you for the rest of your life. It will control you. It will affect everything you do. It will damage every relationship you are in. It will affect the people that you love. It will affect your children and grandchildren. If you do not let it go, you are allowing your pain and its consequences to move on to the next generation. If that happens, it is your fault and nobody else's. Let it go and move on.

The difference between the people in the third category versus the first and second categories is that the third category people take that anger and turn it into a driving force. They bottle it up and use it as fuel, or motivation, to push themselves past what most people are willing to do. It is not a *want* to succeed in their mind. It is a *need* to succeed.

There is a story of a very successful and wise old man who meets a younger man who asks him for advice on **what it takes to succeed**. The old man says, "You want to know what it takes to succeed?" and the younger man says, "Yes, more than anything." So, the old man says, "Follow me." They walk a ways down to a nearby lake, and the old man tells the young man to get in the water about shoulder deep. The young man is confused but listens to the old man. Once they are out there, the young man says, "Why are we in the water? I want to know what it takes to succeed, not how to swim." The old man tells the boy to put his head underwater. The young man is confused but says, "Okay," and obeys. Once his head is underwater, the old man grabs his head and holds it down. After about a minute, the young man needs some air and tries to come up. The old man holds his head underwater even harder. The young man struggles and tries to get away. But the more he struggles, the more the old man holds on even tighter. After about another minute, the young man is going crazy. *This guy is trying to kill me;* he thinks and starts fighting with all his strength. The old man keeps holding him underwater while the boy fights and fights. The young man is beyond panic and is about to pass out when the old man pulls him up. The young man is coughing and gasping for air...and starts yelling at the old man. "What the hell is wrong with you? You're trying to kill me... All I asked for was some advice!!" He screams while still choking. The old man looks at the young man and says, "You asked me what it takes to succeed...and I gave you your answer. When you want success as bad as you needed to breathe just now, that's when you will have it."

These third category people have a need that burns in their soul and drives every waking moment of their lives. It is a powerful thing. If harnessed, it can move mountains.

"The downside of that burning desire is that in many cases, including my own, people can sacrifice anything and anyone—including family—that stands in their way."

I sacrificed my family, and, most definitely, my marriage. At one point, way before any of the success that was to come, I remember sitting in a car outside my apartment at Ohio State University with my mother. I was about to move to Georgia and wanted to see her before I left. We had just gone to lunch and were sitting in the car talking. I was telling her about what I wanted to do and about the plans I had for my life.

I remember her telling me as I sat there, that I should lower my expectations in life. After all, as she said, "You are probably not going to be successful or rich like you want." She went on to say, "You just don't have what it takes to do anything big." I remember being hurt by those words, and I replied, "I will be rich and successful. I don't care what it takes, and I don't care what I have to do, or who I have to step on to get there. I will make it."

I was very angry with her over that conversation. She didn't believe in me. She didn't think I could do it. But she was my mother and was supposed to believe in me. I hated her for not believing in me. My dreams and desire burned inside me like an out-of-control fire. But we will also get to that story later.

For now, here is the lesson.

Believe in your kids — even if their ideas are crazy. Even if you don't really believe in them — do it anyway. Encourage them. Support them. What is the worst that can happen? They'll try and fail, sure, but they will still know that if they want to try something else, you will be there to believe in them again.

On the other hand, the best that could happen is they succeed as I did. You don't want to be the parent whose child is mad at you after they succeed because you didn't believe in them along the way. You also don't want to be the parent whose child doesn't succeed and who loses all hope because you didn't believe in them either. They will hate you for that as well.

CHAPTER 4

I WAS A HAMMER

"If you only have a hammer, you tend to see every problem as a nail." ~Abraham Maslow

I was all-in for this success thing, ready to beat the world into submission.

I had no idea how I was going to get there, but I knew I would find a way because I was on a mission.

The challenge with "all or nothing" thinking is that while the burning desire is an absolute must for the eventual accomplishment of a worthwhile goal, the methods and personal sacrifice can take a toll on everything else that should have meaning in your life. If you allow it to take over, the drive will replace everything else you should hold near and dear. In my case, my desire was born and driven by hate; nevertheless, I didn't really understand that at the time. All I knew was that I wanted money and things and that I had something to prove. I wanted to win the game of life. And I was going to prove it to everyone who thought I would never amount to anything: my parents, teachers, and friends. I would prove them all wrong. There was a HUGE hole in my heart and soul, and I thought filling it with money and success would make me happy. I was in a daily fight for my soul, against everything and everyone, for over thirty years.

It wasn't until my divorce and subsequent therapy that I realized the biggest person I was fighting against, the person that I had to prove myself to, was not the stepfather I hated, or the world I thought was against me. It wasn't my teachers who failed me in class, or anyone else I assumed was making fun of me behind my back and judging me. The person I was fighting against was me. I was battling my own self-image.

I came to realize that I hated myself as much as I hated my stepfather, the world, and everyone else. It was me who thought I wasn't worthy. It was me who had to prove to myself that I was not the loser I was told I was when I was a child. Everything in my life was a battle against a faceless enemy, and everyone else in the world was in my way. I came to realize, however, that the enemy I was fighting was in my heart and soul. When I finally met my enemy face to face, I found out that it was me the whole time. I didn't like me, and I needed to prove to myself that I was worthy.

Before my eventual realization, I was a force to be reckoned with. If you knew me or worked for me, you probably didn't like me. I was as direct as they come. I frequently yelled at people and was mean to my employees if they didn't instantly comply with my instructions. I was short with and yelled at my wife. I should have been treating her as my wife and not like one of my employees. Back in the day, I saw this quote, and it fit me perfectly:

"When you are a hammer, everything else is just a nail." I was a hammer...

And here is the lesson...

Being a hammer isn't necessary. It may work to resolve whatever immediate issue you are facing, but the devastation you will leave behind in your life and in other's lives is not worth it. I had no friends when I was a hammer. I wasn't succeeding as I wanted, and I wasn't a good husband...I was a mess. I was not happy, and it took a lot of years, a lot of failures, a lot of lawsuits, and a lot of sleepless nights to get past that. And it took finally meeting another man I could look up to, who showed me how to be a businessperson without being a complete jerk. That's when my life really started improving...but we will get to that story later as well. In the meantime... I was a hammer.

CHAPTER 5

WOULD YOU CHANGE IT?

"Your past does not determine who you are.
Your past prepares you for who you are to become."
~Unknown

From as far back as I can remember, and until I was about forty-seven years old, I lived my life in the third person—rarely ever-present. As I am fifty-five years old now, the change in me is very recent. It's kind of hard to describe the way I lived and operated. It was as if there was the physical me that was living my life, and then there was this other me up on a balcony in a safe place watching my life unfold and directing the action. I have been told that I removed who I am from my physical body to protect myself from what happened to me as a child. This is a protection mechanism. Unfortunately, though, as an adult, I continued to operate this way. This was not an intentional thing. It was simply the only way I knew how to exist—always in protection mode.

As a side note, being in this detached mode also affected my personal relationships and my marriage. Because I was afraid of getting hurt, I kept everyone at arm's length, including my wife. I do not believe I was capable of giving or accepting love during this time. In my warped mind, love was the ultimate way to hurt someone. If I admit I love you, and then you don't love me back, that is the pain I had as a child. That is the pain I didn't want. Because I didn't feel worthy, I never felt like I was the best option for my wife. I thought she would eventually leave, and I didn't want to feel pain like that coming from the person I loved. Now I know today that feeling this way is an obvious reference to my mother, but back then, all I knew was that I didn't want to get hurt by love again. So I rejected it and was as cold as they come.

As long as I sat up there as that third person on my balcony, nobody could get close to me to hurt me. There was no other basis or role model in my life to guide me. I just didn't know any better. I could have an entire conversation with someone, and at the same time, be watching myself as a silent critical observer, a person completely separate from the one talking. I would analyze myself, the other person, and the conversation while I had it. I know that sounds weird and hard to understand, but it's the way I was. I was highly dysfunctional.

"I rarely ever felt like I was existing in the first person."

I rarely ever connected with anybody one on one unless I needed or wanted something. If I did connect, it was with a purpose and sometimes a vengeance. Making eye contact was only done as an intentional act. It was never casual. That's because making eye contact was intense for me. It was as if eye contact connected me to that person, and I didn't like connection. I had to lower the protective walls that surrounded my inner being to do it. At the same time, while the walls were being lowered, I was also backing them up with another wall of rage and fire. All that anger, hate, and rage from my childhood was like a volcano of emotional power that I kept locked away in a box deep down in my subconscious. This was my anger box. Later in life, I learned that it was also the source of my internal power.

I rarely opened the lid on that box, and if I did, I only cracked it open to let a little fury out. My anger was like fuel for a purpose. The more I let it out, the more fuel poured onto the fire, and the harder I drove toward whatever goal I had at the moment. I tried not to let my anger out very often. Mostly because I was afraid of it and the person that it turned me into. I was afraid of what I was capable of doing if it was unchecked. Imagine a raving lunatic with no pressure gauge or filter. The times that it did get out, I was not a very nice person and was very good at verbally and mentally destroying someone. This was a trait I learned growing up. It was not something I knew that I was learning as a child, but that isn't the way it works with children. They learn the good, and they most definitely learn the bad. The thing is, children don't even know they are learning it. They are just living their lives and absorbing what is going on around them. They are innocent of the long-term effects being programmed into their brains that will shape their future lives and how they deal with other people. I had eighteen years of experience learning exactly how to mentally hurt people, and I was good at it.

Rage as a tool...

Over the years, I learned to use that rage inside of me as a tool, even though early on, I didn't know I was doing it. My responses to people and situations came purely through luck and trial and error, as I learned and grew in the business world. Eventually, I started to understand what I was doing and moved that mental tool to a more conscious level. I figured out how to actively and selectively use rage as a tool for my benefit. It wasn't until years later that I began to understand just how destructive what I was doing was to my employees, family, and friends. My approach worked, but it came at a cost. The problem I struggled to overcome was limiting that particular tool to business situations only. I also used it with people that I shouldn't have.

If I needed to get in a one-on-one situation with somebody, if I needed to bend their will or get them to concede, I could crack the lid on that box just enough to let a little intensity out. Then I could look straight into their soul and go to work. My intensity was very powerful and persuasive as long as I could keep it in check. I learned that I could make people do things and that there is a fine line between pushing people in the direction you want them to go and pushing too far. Walking that line is something every great salesperson can do instinctively. And as I learned in 1997, when I was talked into selling insurance for the first time...

I could sell... I could persuade...or I could mentally bully. As my friend John said, "In a sales situation, you can lock into a group and make people move in the direction you want them to go." I don't know why or how I have that ability—but it's there. The problem was I also did this at home.

Throughout my adult years, I stayed in the third-person mode. I was not social and didn't like to go out with people. There were basically three different times when I would switch to what I called my "first-person mode."

1. In a sales situation

2. If I needed or wanted to punish someone

3. If I wanted to flirt or for sex

Most other times, I was disconnected mentally from the world and the people around me. I was emotionally unavailable. I would be this driven person at work, controlling a room full of people, making them like me, and then come home and not want to talk or make decisions of any kind. I was unsociable. I just didn't like people. I would go to a party, then stand in the corner and leave early because I was bored and didn't like anybody there. I was two totally different people—on or off. Living this way, unfortunately, cost me forty years of happiness and a marriage.

Today I am learning to connect. It's a journey that I have to mentally make myself work on daily. I am learning to use my intensity for happiness, having fun, and making friends instead. I still use it for other things, too, but living happily is much more fun and enjoyable.

So the question is if my negative background and the anger box gave me the ability and drive to succeed and to have the success and material things I have today...was it worth it?

And the answer is...

On the one hand, I have business and financial success. I can do almost anything I want. I can do things that ninety-nine percent of people will never have the opportunity to do. On the other hand, I was not happy most of the time. My inability to connect emotionally with my wife ultimately cost me a happy life and my marriage.

People often ask me if I could go back and change it, would I? The answer to that is simple… Yes. I would trade what I have today for being happy growing up and knowing how to be happy as an adult.

But that wasn't my journey. I was dealt the hand I was dealt. And I did what I knew how to do with it. Hopefully, this book can keep someone else from failing in so many areas of their life the way I did.

If I knew then what I know now and if I had the option, I would've done almost everything in my life differently. I would have finished college. I would have gone to law school. I would have been an officer in the Air Force, and most likely, a pilot. These are my regrets and non-option dreams I would have pursued if I could have changed my path. I would be a totally different person.

But we can't go back, and we can't change things. All we can do is learn to move on with the rest of our life and do things right from here forward. This is a life lesson I wish I could pass on to the kids I see growing up today who so desperately want the things that I have. In their minds, they are willing to do anything and everything to get what they want. I can so clearly see their future. But unfortunately, I have also learned that people don't take advice. Even when they ask you for it, thank you for it, and promise they will take it, they won't. At best, they will take some of it, but then they will change or ignore small parts of what you've told them to do because, ultimately, they believe they know better.

This lesson reminds me of something my daughter once said to me. She was telling me about something she wanted to do, and I was telling her that it was not a good idea, that she should listen to me and learn from my mistakes and not her own. I insisted that learning from other people's mistakes is a better way to learn than just failing. But then she spoke back to me, and I can never forget her words. She said, "Daddy, I think I need to learn the hard way. Otherwise, how am I ever going to know better?" That is a very hard thing to hear as a parent. Yes, I like her independence and willingness to try. But watching your children screw up and fail is hard. I think it hurts me as much as it hurts them.

So here is the lesson...

I had to come to terms with the fact that it would be okay to let my daughter fail. I would have to stand back and watch it unfold and be far enough away that she felt like she was on her own and making her own decisions. But I would still be close enough to catch her when she fell. My job as her father was to pick her back up and send her on her way, hopefully, smarter, wiser, and only bruised, not broken. That is a tough task to do. I hope my children learn this lesson and practice the same patience I have exercised with them with their own children.

CHAPTER 6

MY FIRST PERSONAL GOALS

"Be stubborn about your goals and flexible about your methods." ~Unknown

I grew up in Canal Winchester, Ohio, a very small town. We moved to this town when I was in the third grade after coming from a school where I had a lot of friends and was popular (if you can be popular in the third grade, that is). Right out of the gate in this new school, things went downhill. I was picked on and got into a lot of fights. I didn't really have any friends, and that did not change as I grew up there. Between my home life and my school life, I was a very unhappy child.

Our entire school had about 1000 kids with kindergarten through 12th grade in the same building. My graduating class had about eighty-four people, and I like to joke that I graduated in the top ten percent of the bottom ten percent of my class. This was not because I was not smart. It was purely because I did not care.

**"By the time I was in the seventh grade,
I was on the brink of failing out of school."**

So, the teachers and my parents decided to have me tested to see if I had a learning disability.

On the day I was tested, I sat in a room all day with this lady who had me doing all sorts of random things. I did block puzzles and timed math problems. She had me doing reading comprehension as well as answering general knowledge questions. Most of the tasks seemed pretty random. But it was better than being in class, so I played along. When the session was over, the lady told me that I had an IQ of 135. I was smart but had an attitude problem.

I was angry and scared and had no idea how to function normally. Somehow nobody ever thought to try and figure out why that was. Nobody ever asked what the problem might be, not even my parents. I suppose they just figured my low grades were my fault and not worth trying to fix. But I did learn as an adult that I am very ADHD. It wasn't really a thing back then like it is today.

My attention span on a single subject can be limited. If I am really interested, I can focus. But if not, my attention is on everything else around me and not on what I'm supposed to be doing. Looking back, I know this made learning difficult. Interestingly enough, this has actually served me well in the business world. I can focus at a high level on multiple companies while having the people who work for me manage the details. This allows me to see and process a lot more information than most people who are singularly focused.

So here is the lesson:

Whatever your issue is, it doesn't have to slow you down. You only need to learn to focus on your strengths. Then strive to understand your limitations and find the right tool or bring in the right person or people to handle what you can't or don't want to do. As I like to say: "I have people, and they do the actual work. I am just flying around at 30,000 feet, managing the big picture."

I honestly don't remember ever doing homework in high school. There were many times during high school that I actually forgot where my locker was located and what the combination was because I never went to it. I didn't take books to class and rarely paid attention. I was that kid in class with his head down, sleeping, who the teachers hated. I skipped class forty-two of the first ninety days of my junior year of high school, as I mentioned. I just didn't go to school. My parents were not there when I woke up, so I slept in and showed up when I felt like it. They had no idea what was going on, and I didn't think they cared about my education. I can't imagine not knowing my kids had skipped half their days of school!

When I think back today, it seems like I gave up on school by about the sixth grade. I didn't like school; I didn't like people, and I didn't care. I remember thinking about dropping out after the eighth grade since I had learned that was the age I could do it legally. The only reason I stayed in school after the eighth grade was because I was in the band and on the track team. My band director, Joe, in junior high, believed in me. He was nice to me. I'd never experienced such kind treatment before. I liked it. As it

41

turned out, playing in the band and being on the track team were my first real goals in life. I wanted to succeed, and I was driven—which made me work and focus.

Life lesson here...

Having specific goals can change your life. They changed mine in the eighth grade, and I didn't even understand the power of goals back then. Today, I understand that goals are powerful, and that writing them down is even more powerful. I've written down my goals for the last thirty-five years. I put them in my iPhone in the notes sections. They are written down as short-term, medium-term, and long-term goals that I break down by year. It's amazing how many goals I have accomplished doing this. It really is like magic. You write your goals down, and then your subconscious helps you make them happen.

My first goal in life...

I played the trumpet in the junior high band and was average but not the best. But I didn't care that much and was forced by my parents to practice. The turning point for me came one day when Duane, the kid who was first chair in the trumpet section, got asked to join the high school marching band. I saw him going to marching band practice, and suddenly I felt left out... It was like a switch flipped in my head. Suddenly, I decided that I wanted to be in the high school band. And I thought, *why does he get to go, and I can't?* So I went to the high school band director and asked if I could join the high school marching band. He told me that I was not good enough. When I asked how I could get better, he told me to practice. That was all it took. I had my first goal!

Hearing that made me mad. I couldn't stand it when some-one told me no, that I was not good enough. I decided right then that I would be the best. So I started practicing. Every day after school, I would go to the band room and practice for a couple of hours. And I started taking private lessons, making sure as I practiced that the band director knew I was there. Then I took private lessons from him personally. By the end of eighth grade, I had moved up to first chair in the trumpet section. I had made my goal! I was the best trumpet player in junior high.

The next year as a freshman, I went to the high school band and was placed as the second seat behind a senior. I didn't care if he was a senior; in my mind, he was sitting in my seat, so I worked even harder. By the time I was a sophomore, I was first seat again. It was a small school, but I was the best at something. I liked being the best. However, more importantly, I had figured out how to get what I wanted. I was not a natural trumpet player; I just worked harder than everyone else to meet my goal.

Life lesson...

If you want it, you have to work for it. Hard work, persistence, and a burning desire can put you on an even playing field with people who have natural talent. You may have to work harder than someone else to get what you want, but you can still get it if you want it bad enough. You can do almost anything you want if you are willing to put in the effort, focus and take the time necessary to do it...even if you have to start from the bottom... And if you need motivation and can't find it, maybe you need to get mad!

I watched my son learn this lesson in high school while he was learning to play the guitar. He started taking lessons early but eventually quit. Then one day, he picked the guitar back up and started teaching himself. I asked, "Do you want lessons again?" But he said no. He wanted to do it himself. I was so proud of him for that. I have watched him develop a passion for playing. I have also watched him learn what it takes to become better at what you're passionate about. Along with the guitar, he now plays the piano, the flute, and the drums. He has produced his first 5-song EP and is a pretty good songwriter. My hope is that he will continue. Not just because he will become a better musician—that is truly the least of the benefits he is gaining. What I really hope is that he learns the lesson about what it takes to get what you want. That is the lifelong benefit to what he is doing if he continues down the path he is on. But at this point, all I can do is hope, because much like advice, trying to tell your children things sometimes just doesn't work. They have to learn on their own. So I support and encourage him as I applaud each success along the way.

My second goal was attained one day in the spring when I was outside our high school at the track field. I was watching this guy practice pole vaulting along with a group of kids. It was the coolest thing I had ever seen. Everyone who was watching thought he was so amazing. All it took was watching that guy, and then I knew I wanted to be a pole vaulter. Oh, and by the way, as you can probably anticipate, I wanted to be the best.

Unfortunately, I wasn't that good. So once again, I practiced. I had no natural talent, but for four years, I worked harder than anyone else on our team. For three of those years, I was not good, but I kept practicing. By my senior year, I was practicing up at Ohio State with a friend of a friend who was also practicing for the Olympics. I would drive up there during the summer and practice with him on Saturday mornings, and he would coach me. By the time track season came around my senior year, I was the best in our league. It took me four years of hard work to get there, but I became the best. I liked being the best and winning. It felt so good. I have carried that feeling of accomplishment with me throughout my life. That was a feeling I craved and would work for.

"It gave me a work ethic that others didn't have."

I often wonder if I had not experienced these little successes early on if I would have the work ethic and drive that I have today. At that time in my life, I had nothing else going for me, but in these two areas, I was the best.

I now ask myself, if you never knew what it was like to win back then, would you have even tried as an adult?

The lesson...

It's important to show, teach, and help your children experience success, so they understand what it feels like to be good at something — so they learn what it's like to succeed. They need that feeling. It drives them to bigger aspirations in their future.

45

These two personal goals kept me in high school. I wanted to be the best, so I worked as hard as I could until I was. It was also that one teacher who took an interest in me in band because he made me believe I could do it. He had no idea how important he was in my life at that time.

Life lesson...

You have no idea what impact or influence you may have on someone. They will probably never tell you either. It may be positive or negative. Your influence may save their life or steer them in a direction that will change their life. Always be aware of the influence you may have on other people. You may not even know that people look up to you and watch your actions. But they do.

CHAPTER 7

IN THE BEGINNING

"Childhood is a promise that is never kept."
~Ken Hill

From the time I was about one year old until I was nine, we lived in a suburb of Columbus, Ohio, down the street from the elementary school I attended. All the kids on the block walked to school every day and then walked home after school was over. My parents worked, so after school, I would walk over to the neighbor's house, and the teenage boy and girl there would babysit me until my parents got home. I can't remember her name, but his name was Carl, and he was around fifteen years old. I was seven years old at the time—too young to understand any of what went on at their house at the time, but Carl was a child molester, and I was his victim. Carl told me never to tell anyone about what happened, or bad things would happen to me, so I never did.

Not until after my divorce and I was in counseling did I ever tell a single soul what happened during those years. I often wonder what happened to Carl. *Was he a victim as a child? Did he continue molesting boys? Did he ever get caught? Did he become a Catholic priest...or is he still a predator walking around out there?* I even wonder if I should feel guilty for not following up earlier in life to see if I could stop it from happening to another child.

Life lesson...

You need to be very protective of your children, know who you are leaving them with, and talk to them about what happens in their life. You need to understand that there are very bad people in the world, and your job as a parent is to keep them safe to the best of your ability. In forty years, you do not want to read about horrible things that happened to your children that they never told you because they were afraid!

Carl's mistreatment of me ended when I was nine years old, and we moved to Canal Winchester, Ohio, a small town outside of Columbus. I was raised out in the country on 2.5 acres of land about six miles outside of town. It was a very middle-class life. We were surrounded by farms and could smell the pigs down the road if the wind blew the right way. We went to the lake on the weekends in the summer. Every year we took a hot, miserable drive to vacation in Mississippi at my grandparents' house for two weeks when the plant my parents worked at shut down for the summer. Life continued to move on like that for the next several years.

Both my mother and my stepfather worked full-time and were never home during the day. Back then, people called kids like us who stayed home alone, latchkey kids. During the school year, my parents were gone before I got up to go to school, and nobody was home when I got back. I read an article in the news the other day about some parents who were arrested because their 12-year-old son came home early from school and couldn't get in the house, so he shot basketball for 45 minutes in the driveway until they got there. From the age of about nine, I was on my own every day until nightfall when my parents got home from work. And I was home by myself all day in the summers. That was my everyday life back then. Today, my parents would be arrested for child abuse for allowing that, but the seventies and eighties were a different time.

As a child, I was given lots of chores to do. I had to mow the grass every week. That was a 4.5-hour task on the weekends in the summer. I had to weed the 1500-square foot garden and pick the vegetables when they were ready. I hated it. In the winters, I had to shovel snow and cut and haul wood for the wood-burning fireplace. My stepfather and I would drive around and find open wooded land and then drive into the woods in the truck and cut up dead trees. My job was to carry the wood back to the truck while he ran the chainsaw. This killed a lot of weekends for me. We would typically put up about fourteen cords of wood for the winter. Once we got it home, I was tasked with unloading the truck, splitting the wood, and stacking it on the porch. I spent a lot of time with either an ax or a sledgehammer and a steel wood splitter.

> ## "At the age of fourteen, I was told
> ## I needed to get a job."

So I started bagging groceries at the local grocery store after school for tips. I was too young to be on the payroll, so I was only allowed to make tips when I worked. I was not happy at this age.

Middle and high school were a miserable time for me. We have all heard that it is the best time of your life, but this was not the case for me. When I turned sixteen, I had three jobs. I was told that a job was more important than school or outside activities. Even though I wanted to play more sports and do other things in my free time, the answer was "No. You have to work." And if school got in the way, my job came first. So I worked... I needed money for a car and to buy other things to support myself as well.

School of Music

In my junior year of high school, I thought that music would be my future since I was a pretty good musician for a sixteen-year-old. I'd heard of a school where you could study music all day instead of normal school subjects. That sounded like heaven to me. I applied and was accepted to Fort Hayes School for the Performing Arts. I was excited about the opportunity to be at Fort Hayes and pictured myself working in a career as a studio musician. Doing that would not require me to have a regular job. The hours were flexible, and the pay was good. It was the opposite of what I was told by my stepfather that I should do. So, I showed up the first day at Fort Hayes, excited about my future as a musician. I was surrounded by all these kids who had the same dream

I had. There were actors, dancers, musicians, singers, radio, and TV performers. It was all very exciting; that is until reality set in.

The plan was to attend my regular school for two periods a day. Then I would leave and go to Fort Hayes for the rest of the day. For the most part, I never actually attended my regular school; I skipped those classes, got up late, and went to Fort Hayes. Since I didn't have any parents around, nobody knew.

It didn't take me long to figure a few things out. Some kids in this school were truly amazing, gifted with God-given talent. They had talents I had never heard of like perfect pitch and a perfect ear. They didn't have to read music but could simply listen to a song once and then play it perfectly on the piano, the guitar, or the violin. I was in awe and amazed.

A piano player named Doug could read a book in one hand and play any song I could think of with the other...and never stop reading. One of my good friends, Tim, couldn't read music at all. He just needed to hear it. Tim sat behind me in jazz band and played the bass guitar. If we got a new piece of music to play, he would lean forward and ask me to hum it to him. After I did, he would then lean back and play it perfectly, with a big smile on his face, while he pretended to read the sheet music so the instructor wouldn't know.

There are truly gifted people in the world. They have amazing talents that they never had to work for. I can't even imagine what it would be like to do the things they do. They are special. These kids could play multiple instruments. They could sing and dance and act. I came to realize that they were light years ahead of me and that it was going to take an enormous amount of work to level that playing field. I also came to the realization that they would not all make it. Most of them would become starving artists. In fact, I still know a lot of the kids in my class, and none of them ever became famous. These people were amazing... gifted...special...and it wasn't enough.

Before my junior year was over, I decided that the amount of work I would have to do in music school was more than I was willing to commit to. So I went back to my regular high school for my senior year. My dream was dead.

If there is a lesson here, I think it is this...

Sometimes you have to adjust your goals midstream. Sometimes you have to come to the realization that maybe the path you are on is not the best path for you. Just because you started in one direction doesn't mean you have to finish it. If you find out that the end is not going to be what you want, it is okay to change your goal. I'm not saying that you should make this decision lightly, but sometimes you do need to quit, change direction, and find a new path. I see far too many budding young or old entrepreneurs who are stuck with their vision. They can't see past the fact that their dream isn't working, and they continue down the same path of failure until it's too late. Then they blame fate, bad luck, or the fact that they "just can't catch a break." Sometimes you need to improvise and adapt, change direction, and find another way. "Don't let your vision blind your common sense."

CHAPTER 8

MY FIRST BUSINESS

"I owe my success to having listened respectfully to the very best advice, and then going away and doing the exact opposite." ~G.K. Chesterton

My grandparents lived in Mississippi. My family and I would visit them in the summers for a week or two. It was a long hot ride in the back of a station wagon with no air conditioning, and the car would overheat a lot. We would carry a couple of gallons of water to pour in the radiator when it got too hot. For several summers, when I was between 8-12 years old, I stayed in Mississippi after my family left. I felt safer there. Nobody was going to hit me. I loved those summers in Mississippi. I honestly can't tell you what the stronger pull for me to stay in Mississippi was: whether it was the love of my grandparents, or the safety of not being around my stepfather for a couple of months.

My grandfather was a character. He had a third-grade education and was as redneck as they come…and unfortunately, just as racist. He wore overalls and cowboy boots every day. In the summer, he may or may not have had a shirt on. He called me "Bryant." I'm not sure where the "T" at the end came from, but according to him, that was my name. I remember every morning he would get up and yell… "BRYANT…you comin' or what?" I would say yes, get dressed, and go to the kitchen where my grandmother would have some food heated up for us—usually cheese biscuits and coffee or tea. We would eat that up, then get in his pickup truck and head out.

"My grandfather was an entrepreneur."

He owned several businesses, and one of them had a bunch of bulldozers that his company used for land moving work. He had a used car lot, or maybe two, and bought and sold heavy equipment at auction. Grandad also had a pay fishing pond behind his house, as well as a restaurant. I loved that house and that pond. I remember when I would stay there, he would get up every morning and go "read the wells" since he apparently had a contract with an oil well company to get the readings on the wells every day and send it into them.

I had no idea what the word "entrepreneur" meant, but I LOVED what my grandfather did. He didn't have to get up and go to a job. He set his own hours and made money based on actions and skill as opposed to clocking in and getting a fixed dollar wage per hour. My future was being shaped; I wanted to be like my grandfather. I didn't understand it back then but spending time with him planted a seed in me that never went away. It was the beginning of my future business endeavors. My grandparents had a beautiful house in Mississippi with lots of cars (including a 1965 Jaguar that he told me was mine when I turned sixteen), trucks, and motorcycles. Everyone in town knew him as Junior. I was known as Junior's Grandboy when I was there in the summers.

Life lesson...

Again... *You don't need an education, or a head start of any kind to be successful. You just have to work and figure it out along the way.*

My grandfather was always hustling. That was my favorite thing about hanging out with him. I never knew what we would do next. Any new idea he could think of to make money, he would try. Unfortunately, he also didn't have the greatest moral compass.

One summer, when I was about sixteen, somebody talked him into buying a couple of airplanes and learning how to fly. So he taught himself how to fly off a dirt road in a little Cessna. Then he and another guy took those airplanes down to Mexico to pick up a load of marijuana. They got caught by the DEA on the way back. My grandfather would eventually end up in prison for about two years for drug smuggling. My grandmother lost everything, including the house...and my Jaguar. She had to move to Ohio to be near us to survive. That was tough to watch.

"I visited my grandfather once while he was in prison. It was very hard to see my hero in that place."

I still loved him, but it was a blow to me. He got caught up trying to make fast money and paid the price. After he got out, he moved to Ohio. The rest of his life was a struggle and sad to see. Grandad passed away several years after that. He was driving to church when his car stalled. He got out and climbed under it to see what the problem was but had forgotten to put the car in park. It rolled and pinned him, and he died. He never knew the influence he had on me—never knew that he was a big part of setting my life in motion. I was never that successful when he was alive. But he was my hero as a child, and my memories of him always make me smile. I loved my grandfather.

Looking back, I have to assume that my grandparents were probably not the best parents. This is probably why my mother raised me the way she did. What's interesting is something my daughter said to me. She said, "Grandma's parents were not good parents, and yet you loved them and loved being with them. Grandma was not the best mother, but I love her and love being with her." I thought about that for a minute and agreed with her. My mom is a great grandparent. Isn't it strange that moving from parents to grandparents can change the dynamic of the person so much?

Life lessons...

1. *We already covered this one, but it's worth repeating. You never know how you are influencing the people around you. These could be your friends, children, or even a stranger. Your life reverberates through a lot of people, good or bad. Try to make it good.*

2. *If you were not the best parent, being a grandparent is your shot at redemption. Take advantage of it.*

After watching my grandfather all those years, I have to assume that his self-employed lifestyle had rubbed off on me, even though I hadn't realized it yet.

I started my first business in the eighth grade, although I didn't know it was a business. It wasn't until years later, as I started to piece my life together that I understood the journey that I was on. It wasn't so much a business as a hustle.

I liked candy. Pretty much all kids like candy. There were no vending machines at my school in eighth grade. There was, however, a laundromat in our town that had a box of candy behind the counter that you could buy while you were doing your laundry. I can't remember how I discovered this, but there it was. The candy was twenty-five cents. Each day I got one dollar to buy my lunch at school. And each day after I got to school, I would run down to the laundromat about two streets over and buy candy for a quarter each. Then I would take the candy back to school and sell it for fifty cents each. That was a pretty cool feeling because even back then, I liked "the deal." I liked the kill of making a sale and a profit. So every day after buying and selling, I made a 100 percent profit and ended up with two dollars. I thought that was the coolest thing. As long as the other kids did not know where I got the candy from, I had a lock on the candy market at double the price. Eventually, my best friend figured out what I was doing and tried to cut himself in on the deal. He wanted to pool our money, sell more candy, and split the profits. I said no. I wasn't the best businessman at the age of fourteen, but still wanted to do it solo. Instead of giving up, he competed with me. One thing led to another; the other kids figured out where we were getting our supplies, and my budding little business failed. Soon enough, the kids all got their own candy, and I was out of business. That was my first experience with business cycles, competition, friends, and money.

And here is the lesson...

You have to constantly improvise and adapt, or today's success will be tomorrow's failure. Every good idea will be copied by someone else, and they will probably do it cheaper than you or put you under just for spite.

CHAPTER 9

HIGH SCHOOL AND...I CAN SELL

"I always think the best thing about high school is that it's so many years ago." ~Kaye Morgan

During my junior year, while I was attending the school for the performing arts, I had to take two classes at my regular high school: Typing and World History. As I said earlier, I basically skipped these classes. You could never get away with how many days I missed today. Back then, however, records were kept on paper in a file. Our school was small. There were only three people in the office: the principal, vice-principal (who never looked at the files), and the secretary. The school secretary was Sara, who had a daughter named Sonya. Sonya had a crush on me, and because of this, Sara never reported my absences to anyone, not even my parents. I was missing from school fifty percent of the time, and nobody knew. At the end of the first semester, we had midterm tests. I hadn't been to class very often, so I decided to skip them. Unfortunately, teachers do look at the files after midterms, to do report cards. I was caught. I remember walking into the school the next day on Friday when my track coach saw me and said, "Nice job, dumbass," and walked away. I had no idea what he meant by that until I got called into the office.

The principal took me back to his office and told me he had looked at my files. He could not believe I had skipped so much school and then the midterms. He told me that I would be suspended and have to repeat the 11th grade, or I could drop out. I was also out of the band and dropped from the track team. This was devastating news. As I said earlier, these were the only two things I cared about, and I was not about to lose them.

> **"My mind reeled. I needed to figure out a solution. So I asked the principal what I could do to fix it. He said, 'Nothing. It's over.'"**

I said, "There has to be a solution. I don't want to do another year of school, and you don't want me here." So thinking quickly, I said, "I will make you a deal. I will retake the midterms on Monday. If I get a B or better, you give me a D. If I get less than a B, you can fail me, and I will drop out." The principal was actually a very nice man. He said he would rather I graduate and that he had nothing to lose. He didn't believe I could pull it off over a weekend, so he agreed that I could retake the tests on Monday. The other stipulation was that I couldn't skip school for the rest of that year and my senior year, or the deal was off. I agreed to his terms and left. I had cut my first deal.

Now I had no idea then, but I do believe that was the first time I sold something. I sold myself. I made a deal to stay in school. It's funny looking back at events in your life and not realizing at the time that the seeds of something that would affect your future were there. They were natural and unlearned but still there.

I was desperate and needed to talk my way out of trouble.

It's interesting as I look back on my four careers—most of which have been in sales. I used to tell people our best salespeople were either drunks, or on drugs. They were generally in trouble a lot. I would say, "It's because they have spent so much time trying to talk themselves out of trouble, that they are really good at talking other people into doing things they might not be ready to do."

Oh, by the way... I spent the weekend studying the first two months' worth of material for those two classes. I retook the two tests, and much to everyone's surprise, got a B in both subjects. So, I was allowed to stay in school.

In my senior year, high school did not get any better. I became more distant and angrier as graduation approached. The goal I had pursued in music for the last couple of years was dead. I even dropped out of the high school band because I didn't like the new high school band director. I had a major attitude problem, hated authority, and had no idea what I was going to do after high school. College was not an option. I had no way to pay for it, and I would never get in with my grades. I took the ACT test and got a 12—the lowest grade in my class. I believe you need around a 19 for college. I didn't even bother taking the

SATs. I'd done so badly on the ACT; I figured it didn't matter. To make it all worse, it was made very clear to me that I was "not welcome" in my house. I had to go. But I didn't care. I was ready to leave.

Side note...

My mother and stepfather never pushed me to take the tests. They never pushed me for anything. They didn't seem to care if I failed. They didn't seem to care if I was out getting drunk and driving around at the age of sixteen. I can remember driving home at 80-100 mph drunk at night many times and turning off the lights on my car to see if I could drive in the dark. I didn't care if I crashed. I didn't care if I died. I didn't want to, but I didn't care if I did. I didn't care about anything. I came home many times, hammered drunk in high school, and I know it was obvious. My parents never told me to stop. And they never told me it was wrong as they looked the other way. They basically didn't raise me at all. I was left to make all my decisions on my own.

As a father today, I can't imagine allowing my children to make every decision with no guidance of any kind. They are children. They have no experience in making quality decisions. Kids need guidance. Kids need help. Kids need parents to be parents.

So here is the lesson...

Raise your kids. *Kids want to be raised. They want help. They want your advice even when they fight it. They need you. Yes, you will screw up, and yes, you will sometimes be a bad example. You will even* *give them the wrong advice at times. But that is far better than abandoning their mental and emotional development when they need it the most. Do your best… **Raise your kids**…they are begging for it.*

During the last two years of high school, I worked three jobs at any given point. Some of those jobs included a pizza place, a grocery store, a gas station, a pharmacy, a bowling alley from midnight to eight in the morning doing Saturday night cleaning, working for a local farmer, and as a janitor at a local engineering office at night. I also played a few gigs in a little jazz ensemble at parties.

I did not get any money from my parents. I didn't get anything except clothes when they would buy them for me at the beginning of each school year. That was it. I worked because I didn't have a choice.

My favorite job was at B&K Pizza, where I worked for a guy named Frank and his wife, Eve. I liked Frank. He would always come in the back door of the restaurant and call me Slick. "What's going on, Slick?" It's funny because I say that today to both my kids and the people working for me. Every time I say it, it reminds me of Frank. I remember going back to town a few years after the Air Force to see Frank. By then, he was old, sick, and bedridden. I visited with him one last time. He called me Slick and said he was proud of me for joining the military. I liked Frank even when he yelled at me…and he yelled a lot. But it was always for my benefit and not to hurt me…and I appreciated that. For some reason, Frank liked me. My guess is he understood me.

We were in a very small town with one police chief on the payroll and a couple of volunteer deputies. Frank told me that I had the best job in town. The deputies would come into the pizza place all the time, and Frank would comp them free food. Since I was always working, it was me who gave them the free food. Frank told me that if I ever got into trouble, I should tell the police I worked at B&K pizza. I can't even remember how many times I used that line. It worked almost every time I got pulled over.

Here's the lesson...

Who you know can be just as important as anything else you have going for you. Never underestimate the power of friends. They can make or break you. Networking is a powerful tool in your success. So go make friends and not enemies.

Most, if not all, of the money I made, went to pay for my car. More accurately, my cars.

"Between the ages of 16-18, I had a total of ten cars."

Prior to getting my first car, I used to take my parents' car out and drive it around. They left the keys hanging on a hook in the coat closet. Since they were gone all day at work and I was bored, I took the keys and the car out when I was only fourteen and fifteen. I would drive all over the place before they got home from work. We lived in the country, so there were no police around. I also did this with my stepbrother's silver '68 Firebird. Man, I loved that car.

All of the cars I owned back then were junk when I bought them, and I had to keep putting money in them to keep them running. I could tear apart an engine and put it back together by the time I was sixteen. My first car was a '68 Chevelle SS 396. I blew up the motor in that one while I was still fifteen. Over the next couple of years, I had a '70 Torino GT that I wrecked the first time I ever drove it. I was putting new brakes on it, and my stepfather told me not to drive it until he got home to help me bleed the brake lines. Of course, I didn't listen and drove it to school. My logic was simple; all you had to do was pump the brakes about ten times to get it to stop! This worked great until I had to stop suddenly on the highway, and the car didn't stop. I put it in the guardrail and smashed the heck out of it. Later, I fixed it and then broke the frame in four places trying to jump hills like they did on the *Dukes of Hazard* TV show.

After that, I had a string of cars that I either blew up the engines in or wrecked. I had three Vegas, one of which was just a Vega body on an International Scout chassis with big mudder tires. I wrecked a Ford truck and a Caprice classic. I had a baby blue Monza I borrowed from my parents while one of my other cars was wrecked. But my favorite was a '70 Cutlass 442. It was a rust bucket with a bad interior, but it was fast. I blew up the motor racing it twice before I got my hands on a '68 Firebird just like my stepbrother's. Ironically, I also blew up the motor in that one. I spent a LOT of time in the garage trying to keep these junkers going. I have said many times that I held those cars together with chewing gum and chicken wire.

But the one thing that I would not compromise on when it came to my cars was a killer stereo. Yes, I was one of those kids with a $300 car and a $500 stereo. After I got off active duty in the Air Force, I bought a new car for the first time. It was a little Chevy Chevette. Not a fancy car by any means, but it had a warranty. When I got that car, I decided I would never work on another car as long as I lived. That holds true today.

Life lesson...

Music is important!! Okay, that's not really a life lesson... But still, music is important!!

CHAPTER 10

I GOT HUSTLED

"There are two kinds of people in the world: givers and takers. The takers may eat better, but the givers sleep better." ~Danny Thomas

Remember, I had already been told when I graduated that I was not welcome and had to leave my home.

In my senior year of high school, the stress of graduation was building. I was ready to get out of high school but still had no idea what I was going to do. So one day, I was sitting in the hall skipping class when the school's guidance counselor saw me and came over to talk to me.

She was a nice lady and asked, "What are you doing?" I told her, "I'm skipping class." She then told me that she could not let me do that, and to keep me out of trouble, advised that I should go listen to the Air Force recruiters talk. I laughed and told her that I would never join the military. However, since I did not wish to get in trouble, and she had made the offer, I said I would go.

I remember sitting in a room watching a movie on one of the old movie projectors about basic training and life in the military. The guys in this video were all six feet tall, muscular, and super good-looking. When they smiled, their teeth sparkled. Girls fainted and screamed when they walked by. They were like supermen. I had not dated in high school, and I'm not quite sure what happened during that movie, but when it was over, I knew I had to join the Air Force. I joked later that I was so rebellious and hated authority and being told what to do so much that I was going to live my life my way—so, I left home and joined the military!

When the movie was over, I told the recruiter guy, "Okay, I'm in. What do I need to do?" All the while, I was thinking, *this solves all my problems. I have a place to go. I have a job. I get money. They give me clothes, food, and a place to live. I get away from my overbearing stepfather. This is awesome.*

The recruiter then looked straight at me and said, "I'm sorry, but we don't need you. We are all full up." I was stunned and thought, *he told me I can't do what I want to do? I am not allowed to join the military?* That made me mad.

Life lesson...

This situation reminds me of the takeaway close. I use it all the time in sales. It is an easy way to get someone to demand to take what you are offering. Although, it generally only works on weaker minds...and I was absolutely one of those.

After being blown off, I called the recruiter a few days later. I was not taking no for an answer. This was after telling my mother I was joining the military and her subsequent meltdown and yelling at me for two days. She told me, "There's no way I am letting you go." Hearing this, of course, made me that much more adamant that I was doing it. I told her I could do whatever I wanted, and there was nothing she could do.

Then I called the recruiter and told him I wanted in. To my astonishment, he told me that he had seen my high school transcripts and that he was not interested in me. "There's probably a two-year waiting period anyway," he said. The problem with his statement was, I had already decided that I was getting in. So, we started negotiating. I asked him how I could get around the two-year waiting period and how I could convince him that he should let me in. Now, think about this for a second, this recruiter had *me demanding that he let me in the military!!*

He told me that I would have to take an entrance exam and if I scored high enough that he would consider it. My response was, "When and where?" The recruiter again told me that he had seen my transcripts, and I would probably not pass the test.

"I assured him that I would do well; remember, I had that 135 IQ in my back pocket."

So I took the exams and then got a call a few weeks later from him. He told me that I had scored in the top one percent and could choose any field I wanted. I remember standing in the dining room talking to him on a phone with a super long cord... Yes, we had phones with cords back then.

I asked him what the hardest field was in the Air Force, and he told me Avionics. I had no idea what that was, but it sounded good. So, I told him to sign me up. I ended up in an early placement program, having joined the Ohio Air National Guard during my senior year of high school; I just didn't go to basic training until after I graduated.

Now I would love to tell you that all that happened because of my amazing negotiating skills at the age of seventeen. But when I look back, I'm pretty sure the Air Force got the best of me on that one.

There is, however, a lesson here. *Make sure you're not getting hustled by a smarter person than you!*

CHAPTER 11

I HAVE MADE A TERRIBLE MISTAKE

"And when he gets to Heaven to St. Peter he will tell"
'Just another soldier reporting, sir.
I've served my time in Hell.'" ~The Soldier's Poem

The first day my unit and I got to basic training was an eye-opener. Remember, I was a super rebellious kid with a raging bad attitude and an authority problem. Upon arriving at Lackland Air Force base in Texas, my life changed. We had not even gotten off the bus before we were getting screamed at. I cannot remember what they were yelling at us about; it was just screaming. In the first twenty minutes, we learned things like the "pick it up and put it down" drill, as well as to "NEVER say you're sorry!!" The typical response when someone said that to the drill instructor was, "I know you're sorry, Airman, but I didn't ask you for a personality profile!!"

Soon after we all got our hair cut off, we were issued new clothes and learned how to make a tight bunk—pretty standard military stuff. As we progressed through the first few days, we started to learn the ins and outs of everyday life in basic training.

Drill instructors (DIs) loved to sneak up behind you while you were standing at attention. They would get just close enough for the brim of their hat to touch your head. This, of course, startled you since you were at hyper attention anyway and most likely super tired. Once startled, your immediate reaction was to flinch or turn your head—which would launch the instructors into a screaming fit about something or other. They would then spin around, so they were facing you and yell in your face with spit flying and bad breath. It was terrifying. These DIs hustled us around from one stop to the next, yelling the entire time.

That first night we got to Lackland AFB, they put us to bed at 9 PM and told us we would be up at 4 AM. Like most of the guys in our platoon, I was not able to sleep much. The instructors would randomly walk around the barracks in the middle of the night. They wore metal taps on their shoes so you could hear them coming on the tile floor. You didn't dare open your eyes or look at them. You just had to lie there with your eyes closed, listening to how close they were. If they stopped by your bed, it was nerve-wracking.

We were in a big barracks with bunks lined up next to each other. Everyone was nervous, excited, and scared. Nobody knew what was going to happen. I remember lying there that first night with my shaved head. It felt weird on the pillow. I was used to having long hair. The next morning at 4 AM, we were awakened by a bunch of drill instructors screaming at us to get up. They banged baseball bats on trash cans and lifted our bunks up and slammed them on the ground while screaming in our faces.

"I was so tired from not sleeping that I will never forget my very first thought when I woke up. *Holy shit... I have made a terrible mistake!!!*"

That was not the last time I thought that.

Life lesson and an oldie but goodie...

Be careful what you wish for...you might not like it when you get it.

On day two of basic training, a DI came around and asked us if anybody played an instrument. I was leery of answering because I had been told never to volunteer for anything. A couple of people raised their hands, and the DI told them to step aside. That didn't seem so bad, so I raised my hand, too. I was then told to step aside, and we were sent to an audition for the Air Force drum and bugle corps. I ended up as the featured soloist and lead bugle.

Being in the corps meant that the other Airmen and I got out of a lot of the BS that most people in basic had to go through. We spent a fair amount of time doing parades and practicing for events. Twice a day, I got picked up by a car to go play taps or "Reveille." I also figured out that laundry was the best detail to pull because all you really did was put the clothes or linen in the wash and wait...and then the dryer and wait. Best of all, the pay-phones were in the laundry area so I could sneak calls home—

and they were not allowed! Somehow, I had figured out how to game the system to make my life easier than the rest. This turned out to be a trait I would carry with me throughout life.

Part of our training involved getting a series of shots. Now I was paranoid of needles, so shots were my least favorite thing. I remember one morning when we were all sitting on the ground under this big metal roof facing a stage. The DI was up on stage, giving us instructions on what was about to happen. We were all going to get in line and walk through the next building single file. Stations with medics in each station would give us a shot as we walked by. When you got one shot, then you would walk to the next station and get the next shot and the next until you were done. There were about eight stations in total, which meant we would get eight shots. I was terrified and sweating, wondering if I would pass out in front of all the guys.

The DI then asked if anyone was allergic to tetanus. A couple of guys raised their hands. Someone then asked why the DI wanted to know, and he said, "If you are allergic to tetanus, you can skip that shot." I thought; *I'm down to seven shots instead of eight. This is a good deal.* So I raised my hand. The DI then told those of us who raised our hands that we could skip station eight. Then I thought *I am a genius. I once again figured out how to game the system.*

The next day while we were at drill, I was called out and told to report to the hospital on base. Once again, I thought *not only did I get out of a tetanus shot, but now I get to skip drill. I really am a genius.* So, I go across base and into the hospital, where the nurse tells me to sit down beside another guy in the waiting room. I walked over to see this guy sitting there holding his arm. I asked him what he was doing there, and he told me he was there for tetanus allergy testing.

Now I was puzzled.

I asked him, "What exactly is tetanus allergy testing?" He proceeded to tell me that "They give you a shot every 5-10 minutes for an hour..." Quickly, I did the math and figured out I was going to get eight shots!!! Suddenly I was no longer a genius; I was an idiot!!

Oh, by the way... I'm not allergic to tetanus.

Life lesson...

Come on, man...suck it up... Shots aren't that bad.

"After I left Lackland AFB, I put my trumpet down and never picked it back up. I was on a mission to survive and succeed, and music wasn't going to help me in any way."

So, I dropped it and never thought about it again. I ended up selling my trumpet after I got married because we needed money to buy food. Now, I wish I hadn't done that.

The next eight months were tough. I got through basic training and then went on to tech school. We got yelled at a lot; we drilled; we marched, and we learned. I spent six months at Chanute Air Force Base in Rantoul, Illinois, after Texas. That winter was the coldest I have ever been. We marched forty-five minutes every morning and every afternoon in -15° weather. It was miserable.

Those eight months on active duty left me with four distinct issues that still affect me to this day. 1) I cannot stand the cold. 2) I eat faster than anybody I know. 3) I cannot stand wearing anything with a tight collar or a necktie. That's because I spent too much time standing at attention in a tie on an asphalt pad in 100-degree heat in Texas. And 4) when I get tired, I want to sleep. Now, I can sleep through almost anything since I used to practically sleep and march at the same time.

I learned during that time that you can push your body through much more than you think. Endurance and pain pose more mental barriers than physical. I have used this knowledge frequently in the last several years when I have pushed my body through physical challenges that I did not think I could do.

I used it when I started running in triathlons and when I ran my first marathon a couple of years ago. I also signed up and did the Alcatraz Sharkfest swim in the San Francisco Bay. Eight hundred of us got onto three boats and went around to the backside of Alcatraz Island. We all jumped off the boat and had to tread water until the boats cleared, and then we swam back to the shore in the water park. The 1.5-mile swim was brutal. I was freezing cold and extremely tired. Now, I am not a good swimmer, but I pushed myself through it mentally and finished in just over an hour.

I have run a 70.3 Ironman—which means six hours and fifty minutes of nonstop endurance. At some point, you stop thinking, and you just go like you're on autopilot. I spent eleven hours climbing two 14,000-foot mountains a couple of years ago with my brother-in-law, Matt, including two class three crossings. Your body can go further than you think. It's a mental game of *"will you quit?"* You need to get your mind to stop thinking about quitting so you will just keep moving. Nike got it right... "Just do it."

And there is the lesson...

I promise you can do whatever physical task you want to do if you want it bad enough. When your body says, stop, you need your mind to be strong enough to override the pain to keep going. Train your mind to overcome your body.

After three years in the Ohio National Guard, I transferred to Georgia, where I got my top-secret security clearance and joined a communication squadron at Dobbins AFB. During one of our weekend drills, I was talking to some of the guys and telling them that I would love to fly, but the Air Force wouldn't let me without a college degree. One of the guys told me that the Army would let me fly without a degree. Not only that, but there was a unit right down the runway from where we were stationed that had enlisted flight positions available. I had always wanted to fly, so I took off that afternoon to go see the Army recruiter.

Once again, when I met him, he told me that there was almost no way I would be able to get into the unit. When I asked him why he said, "The test is really hard, and most guys don't pass." *Here we go again being told no.* I didn't accept that, so I asked him if I could take the test. He finally agreed and scheduled me to take it a couple of weeks later.

The day of the test, the recruiter came with me. I went into a room and sat down for the two-hour test. About forty-five minutes later, I finished, turned my test in, and walked out of the room. The recruiter asked me what happened. I was puzzled and said, "What do you mean?" He asked why I had quit and not finished the test. I assured him that I was done with it. He then told me, "Nobody has ever finished that fast," then he walked into the room to check my answers.

When he came back out about ten minutes later, I asked how I did. He told me I had missed only one question on the test and finished in record time. I could see by the look on his face that he was impressed. He told me, "You're in if you want it." I said yes, and the next thing you know, I had transferred over to the Army.

Very few people do multiple services in their life. I was one of them. I loved flying with the Army. It was the coolest thing I had done at that point in my life. The only problem with it was the Army itself. I experienced so many crazy stories that I don't have the time to get into all of them. I got out of the military in the fall of 1991, right before Desert Shield began. I was never activated to go to war in my eight years, but the military did straighten me out a bit. It was good for me. I'm glad I served.

CHAPTER 12

COLLEGE...OR THE LACK THEREOF

"Each moment of our life, we either invoke or destroy our dreams." ~Stuart Wilde

In the spring of 1984, I had just gotten off my initial active duty with the Air Force and was back home with the Ohio Air National Guard. I decided to use my GI Bill and go to college. Because of my initial Air Force training, I had the equivalent of around two years of college credits. This gave me transfer student status, and I was accepted to Ohio State. The Air Force was going to pay my full tuition to finish my degree. What an incredible opportunity I had to turn my life around educationally.

Back to that question of what I would have done differently... I should have taken the free education, but I didn't.

I started off well enough and used my GI Bill to pay my tuition. I also got a student loan for $2500 and had money in the bank. The problem was...I still had a *"desire for things"* problem and no self-discipline.

Don't forget; I didn't have anyone to guide me, or help me make good decisions. So instead of using that loan money to pay for school, I went out and bought a new stereo system and a pair of leather coats for me and my girlfriend (later my wife) as well as a computer to play games on. Then the money was gone.

Now how was I going to pay for my living expenses and stay in school?

Still, I managed to stay in school for a little over a year—changing my degree twice. I even spent a semester as a teacher's intern at an elementary school. Because I spent the loan money, I had to work a full-time job at a bar on High Street called Papa Joe's. So there I was working full-time, taking a full load of classes, dating my first girlfriend, and racking up my JC Penny card. I bought a car I couldn't afford and was in debt, struggling to make all my payments. I was stressed out.

During that year, I met a guy who worked with me. He got me involved in a multilevel marketing company. I joined Amway when I was nineteen, convinced I would be a millionaire in a couple of years.

I was a full-time college student, deep in debt, working at a bar making four dollars an hour, and living with my girlfriend and four other guys while trying to convince people they should join Amway and get rich with me. The truth is that they should not have joined me—because none of us had a prayer of getting rich at that time. But I did learn a lot back then. I never made any money in Amway, but I absorbed more about business, people, and selling than you will ever learn in college. Amway gave me

80

motivational and self-help books to read. I read well over 100 of them in the course of several years—many of them two and three times. They contained positive information I had never heard before, and I soaked it up like a sponge.

That was the first time in my life I was exposed to something positive and people who told me that I could do anything I wanted to do.

I went to seminars and listened to cassette tapes from people who had succeeded in life and business.

"As I had never had any guidance from my parents relating to life, business, or personal management, my time with Amway gave me the desire to be self-employed."

When you combine that with my authority problems, my future was set…I was unemployable. As I said, I never made any money in that business, but I probably made more money from my *association* with that business than anything I've ever done.

Life lesson…

Sometimes what you are currently doing is a stepping stone to the next level. You're not going to start at the top. You need to learn first. Some of us need to learn more than others. Don't waste time complaining that what you're doing isn't helping you. The truth is you are probably learning more than you realize, and you probably need all the help you can get! Enjoy the journey. This is not the last thing you will do. It's just a chapter in your book.

Unfortunately, that unemployable status did not work out for me over the next couple of years. While I was still at Ohio State, I racked up debt...I couldn't pay my bills, and my car got repossessed because I could not make the payments. That was not the last time I had a car repossessed, either.

Then in my infinite wisdom, after a year of college, I dropped out.

This story has a back story. When I enrolled, I had to take English and math placement tests. I took both tests and was shocked when I got a letter from the university telling me that I needed to enroll in remedial Math and English before I would be allowed to start my actual classes. I couldn't believe it but figured the university knew what they were doing, so I went to class. Our math class was so basic we were learning how to use a calculator. We were drawing squares on a page and then putting numbers in them to show that calculators had numbers, and you could press those numbers to do a math equation.

My English class wasn't any better. We started out learning what a highlighter was and had to highlight passages in a book. I'm not kidding. The students in that class really didn't know how to do this. After a week, I'd had enough and went to the admissions department to tell them they'd made a mistake.

The lady in the office insisted in no uncertain terms that "We don't make mistakes, and you belong in those classes due to your test scores." We got into an argument because I would not accept that answer.

She was wrong. I asked her to see my scores. She told me that nobody gets to do that and said I needed to go. I asked her who her supervisor was (a trick I still use today). She said that her supervisor was not in. I said, "That's okay. I will sit here and wait. I'm not leaving until I see her." This clearly upset her, and she left. After about an hour, another lady came in and told me she was the supervisor and that they don't make mistakes. I then got into an argument with her and told her I needed to see my test. If I was wrong, I would go away, but I was not leaving until I saw my scores. At this point, she was standing in front of me with her hand on her hip and anger on her face. I was not listening to her, and I was not leaving. Clearly frustrated and wanting to prove her point, she disappeared. When she returned, the supervisor was in disbelief. This had never happened before, she told me. She couldn't believe it and was so sorry. But yes, my scores were mixed up, and I did not belong in those remedial classes.

My response was, "GREAT! Move me to the right class." But the supervisor then told me I could not get into the correct class because it was too late. My only option was to finish the classes or drop them. If I dropped them, I would lose my GI Bill. So, I was forced to spend a semester taking classes for no credit and for no reason. I had been screwed by the system. What I should have done is gone to see that supervisor earlier when I could have still changed the courses.

Here is the lesson, and this is a HUGE one that I tell my kids all the time. *You do not have to accept an answer that someone else gives you. They are not always right. In general, people do not expect you to challenge them. But if you think you're right, then you should absolutely challenge any answer you don't accept. You do not have to accept NO. You have options.*

I got through the rest of that semester and the next and had started my third semester when the wheels came off the bus. I remember it vividly. I was in English class and had been given an assignment to write a paper. I wrote the paper, turned it in, and got a B. I thought the paper was really good, so I went to see the professor to find out why she gave me that grade. We were sitting in two cubicles in the library when she told me that she did not like my style of writing. I was not happy with that answer and told her that it wasn't fair that she had given me a lower grade purely because she didn't like the way I wrote.

I remember she leaned toward me and said, "Brian, if you are going to succeed in life, you are going to have to learn to jump through some hoops. In this case, you are going to have to jump through mine."

"I was stunned and couldn't believe what she said. My rebellious anti-authority mode kicked in. The lid cracked open on the anger box in my subconscious."

The switch in my brain between rational and irrational tripped. I told her that I would never jump through somebody else's hoops; I would make it in this world on my own and would rather drop out of college than jump through her hoops. She told me that was my choice. So I dropped out of college and moved to Atlanta.

Dropping out of college is one of the biggest regrets of my life. There were a number of years where I was proud of that statement and what I did. Unfortunately, however, it caused significantly more pain and struggle over the next twenty years than I had bargained for. I was rash, unfocused, undisciplined, and lacked any basis to make the statement and the decision that I made. I have paid the price for that decision my entire life.

Here's the life lesson...

It's another big one...and sometimes hard to handle. The world is what it is. You will have to follow the rules if you want to succeed. You will have to absolutely jump through hoops that you don't want to jump through. You can scream about it, cry about it, fight it, and hate it, and it won't change a thing. At some point, you will learn to accept it and play the game within the rules, or you will end your life here on planet earth a failure. Life is not fair. Sometimes life is unjust. The society we live in is not designed for you to succeed. You will have to fight for success. It's not easy. And you are not better prepared, or smarter, than everybody else. Nobody owes you anything. Achieving your goals will not happen quickly and, in fact, will probably take a long time, longer than you want it to take and longer than you thought it would take. The sooner you figure out what you need to do, the sooner you can begin the process of getting what you want in life. Some people figure that out early, some figure it out later, and some never figure it out and spend their life complaining about it.

A quick side note...

I am not talking about the people who have every advantage in the world, the ones with the right parents, background, education, and all the money necessary to do what they want to do. That was not my journey. I am not talking about my children. :-) I am talking about the rest of us—the majority, the ones who don't have what they need, but who want specific outcomes. If that's you, then figure it out, quit fighting your reality, buckle down, start working on you, get ready to fight, and be prepared for the long-haul.

Thousands will start on the road to reaching their dreams...

Hundreds will persevere for a while...

A few will get close...

And a few will make it.

Are you one of the ones who will?

CHAPTER 13

I HATED OHIO...AND FREE RENT

"The struggle is part of the story." *~Whitney English*

Part of my internal need to get away from my life and past stemmed from the desire to leave Ohio.

Now I'm sure there isn't really anything wrong with Ohio, but it represented everyone and everything that I needed to escape at the time. So I left. The first time I moved to Georgia was in 1985. My college girlfriend dropped out of school with me, and we moved down there together.

At the time, I was still with the Ohio Air National Guard as an avionics technician and weekend warrior. When I decided to move, I had to pick a place to go. The National Guard told me I had five options. I could move to Myrtle Beach, South Carolina; Jacksonville, Florida; New Orleans, Louisiana; Hawaii, or Atlanta. Four of those locations were on the beach! My decision came while I was talking about my plans and options with my friend, who lived in Atlanta. As I was talking to him, he suddenly said, "Hey, if you move to Georgia, you can stay with me rent-free, and I can get you a job with my company doing labor making fifty dollars a day!!" My response was, "COOL, free rent. I guess I'm coming to Atlanta." Meaning the last thirty-five years of my life and my children's lives were set in motion because of free rent.

When we moved to Georgia the first time, we had nothing. I didn't even have a car, because it had gotten repossessed. I had to borrow my friend's car to get to work. I wanted to get out of Ohio so badly I didn't care. I called this "breaking the cycle." It was imperative that I disassociated with virtually everything I knew. I needed to start a new way of life, and I knew that if I stayed in Ohio, the pattern would continue. I wanted new patterns for my future family. I knew then that I would not allow my future children to even loosely associate with my past. It was too dangerous, and it was my responsibility to make that change.

Picture yourself as a parent. Your daughter calls you and tells you that she is dropping out of college to move from Ohio to Georgia with a guy who has no job, no place to live, and no car. I can't even imagine what must have gone through Anita's parents' heads. *Our daughter has completely lost her mind!* I'm also pretty sure they didn't like me for stealing her away from them and her future.

After about two months, Anita and I moved out of our friend's place and got an apartment. We had no furniture. We had no pots and pans. We had nothing but the clothes on our backs and a borrowed car. I was still working as a construction laborer, and she had two jobs—one working at Applebee's as a waitress and the other working at a daycare center. Since we only had one car and both of her jobs were about a mile up the street from our apartment, she walked back-and-forth to work, sometimes walking home at 1 AM by herself. I was making sixty dollars a day as a laborer by then, and she was making about the same in two jobs. We were rocking at $600 a week.

"We saved $100 and bought a waterbed. That was the extent of our furniture."

When my mother came to visit, she would sleep in the bed, and we would sleep on an air mattress. We were not your average yuppie power couple. When we went to the grocery store, we took a calculator to add up the cost of everything we put in the shopping cart because we would only have thirty dollars in cash. I can remember many times going over our limit and having to put things back. That is not the best feeling in the world when there's a line of people behind you. Fortunately, Anita got to eat for free at the restaurant, and that helped cut our food bills.

Then one day, I got fired from my construction job and had to walk thirteen miles back to my apartment because she had the car, and I didn't have a phone to call her. I was stopped by the police at one point because they thought I was a homeless vagrant. Welcome to Atlanta.

I then went and got a job as an assistant manager at a Little Caesars Pizza. That only lasted about two weeks because I could not seem to figure out how to make the register balance, and I had no patience for measuring the weight of the ground beef and vegetables. I got fired one night when I called the district manager for his help. I then took a job as a waiter at a restaurant in

Marietta called Brickworks. That only lasted a couple of weeks. I remember working a double one Sunday and being there for twelve hours. At the end of my second shift, I had somehow either physically lost money or didn't collect from a customer. The store policy was that it was my responsibility for the tickets and the money. Since I didn't have enough money to cover my sales, I owed the restaurant money. The owner sat me down and told me that this was probably not the best career for me. I was fired. As an interesting side note, I own a small chain of restaurants today, and at one point, that same guy who fired me applied for a job as a district manager for my restaurant company. I didn't hire him...

After that, I decided to lower my goals and apply to be a busboy at Applebee's, where Anita worked. I got the job. It was the only job I could apparently hold onto. I kept it until we went back to Ohio to get married in June of 1987.

Life lesson...

I am less worried about where you are today and what you're doing than I am about your attitude and ambition. If you can figure out how to get those two factors right, your future is an open book. Where you start has absolutely nothing to do with where you can end up. That is up to you, and nobody else.

CHAPTER 14

WE GOT MARRIED

"Being in a long marriage is a little bit like that nice cup of coffee every morning. I might have it every day, but I still enjoy it." ~Stephen Gaines

Looking back, my wife and I never really had a prayer at a normal life or a happy marriage.

Anita was my first girlfriend. I never really dated anyone in high school and certainly didn't have a girlfriend. I had no concept of what love was. I had no idea what a healthy relationship looked like. The only example of a relationship or marriage I had ever experienced was one of anger and abuse. As a result, I didn't like or trust people and never felt like I was loved by anyone in my life.

We were doomed from day one. We just didn't know it.

When one day, this girl came along and wanted to be with me, I was hooked. Nobody else wanted to be with me, and *she did*. I thought that was awesome.

We started living together after our second date. I figured if she liked me, I wasn't going to let her go. Who knew if another girl would ever like me again? So, we lied to her parents and told them that she lived in another apartment that they paid for at Ohio State. When they would come to visit her, she would go over there and pretend she lived there. Her roommate thought it was awesome—half the rent paid, and she lived by herself.

After about a year of dating and Anita watching me not be able to pay the bills and then get my car repossessed for the first time because I was three months behind in the payments, I decided I was going to move to Georgia. Of course, she was going with me; I was not letting her out of my sight.

So, I convinced her to drop out of school and move with me. I told her she could start back to school once we got down to Georgia. (She went back for one semester and then quit because she had to get a job to help us survive.)

Telling her parents that we were going to move and live together was not fun. Her mother was not having any of it and told me that if we were living together that we were getting married, and I needed to pick a date. I didn't really care about marriage and told her that she and her daughter could plan the wedding, and I would show up.

Here is a very sad thing to say. I never asked my wife to marry me. I am not proud of that. It makes me sad today when I look back at all of the normal life events that people are supposed to go through that I missed.

We never did the whole engagement thing. We didn't do parties or have rings. It was honestly the most pathetic situation you can imagine.

That's why it makes me so happy to see my children experience life the way it's supposed to be experienced—including my daughter, who just got married. I was able to give her an amazing wedding. The entire experience was perfect. I am very proud of that.

In my case, Anita and I got married in Cleveland, Ohio. She and her mother planned everything, and I showed up when they told me to. My parents had absolutely nothing to do with our wedding. At this point, they had forfeited their role and authority as parents, mentors, or confidants, and I was not about to give it back to them.

We left Georgia in the spring of 1987 and moved back to Ohio to get married. The wedding was up in Cleveland, Ohio, where her parents lived. They went all out, and it was actually a nice event. After we got married, however, we had no place to go, so we went back down to Columbus and moved in with my grandmother. She had an empty bedroom, and we needed a place to go. As I said before, I had no job and still didn't have a car.

But luck was about to turn. One day we were hanging out when one of my friends called. He worked for a landscaping company mowing grass and wanted to know if I wanted a job. He told me he would pay me four dollars an hour... in cash!! I took the job.

Life lesson...

Make it a point to do all the things in life that have meaning. I was too angry to care about the little things, and today I regret it.

CHAPTER 15

ONE OF US IS STUPID

"Life is hard, but it's harder if you're stupid."
~Michael Crichton

It is always interesting to look back at the series of events that shaped your life.

You have no idea what is going on at the time, and yet things are happening that will drive you in a direction for decades to come. It isn't until many years later that you can recognize what happened and how it affected you. This chapter recounts one of those times for me.

I went to work cutting grass. It was a no brainer job. You cut the grass, you blow the clippings off the sidewalk and street and trim where needed. Pretty simple. This was a perfect job for me. It didn't require any brainpower...just labor.

We kept a logbook in the truck. After every lawn we cut, we would go up and collect a check and then mark it in the book. Most lawns were $25-35 a week. After about a week, I added up all the checks we were collecting from mowing lawns. The amount was over $2000 a week. I was amazed!! I was making about $200. The guy sitting beside me was making about $250. The guy driving the truck was making about $400 a week. The guy who owned the truck was making about $1000 a week after expenses. The difference was that he was sitting at home in the air conditioning while I was busting my ass in the summer heat. I remember sitting in the truck one day thinking about that arrangement.

"Then it dawned on me like a light bulb going on, or a vision from God: one of us was stupid!! And I knew which one it was."

I talked to the guys in the truck about my epiphany. I explained that we would be much better off doing the work ourselves. I asked them, "Why are we working for someone else?" They both told me I was crazy and that it was not that easy to start a business. They said that I should quit thinking about it and go back to work.

But I couldn't stop thinking about it. I was already a millionaire lawn care guy in my head!! I was already rich!! Maybe I was channeling my grandfather; maybe I hated having a job, or maybe it was that fire in me that I was going to succeed no matter what. But I saw this as the first opportunity that didn't require any brains. I could cut grass!

So I decided to start a lawn maintenance business. Let me remind you that I had absolutely no idea what I was doing and was running off of two weeks of experience. My new wife and I had gotten about $4,800 dollars in cash for our wedding, so I was ready to go on a spending spree for equipment. I took the money and bought a lawnmower, weed eater, and a blower. Then I borrowed a truck and went into business for myself. By now, I didn't have any money left and had no idea what marketing was or how to get customers.

That was okay because Anita and I came up with a plan. I bought a ream of paper and a couple of markers, and we hand-made a bunch of flyers. My new wife and I walked around sub-divisions sticking them in people's mailboxes. After a few weeks, the local postmaster called and threatened to fine me if I did it again. Apparently, it is illegal to put things in mailboxes. How-ever, much like all the people who stick things in my mailboxes today, I didn't pay attention to the postmaster and kept doing it.

Over the course of the summer, we contracted some jobs and made a little bit of money. It was more than four dollars an hour, but we were still not making a lot. After about three months, I was not a millionaire, but I did have a taste for being self-employed.

In the fall of 1987, I decided we needed to move back to Georgia. By this time, I had switched over from the Air National Guard to the Army National Guard and was stationed at Dobbins Air Force Base in Marietta, Georgia. I had a guy work-ing for me at the time. He was my best friend from college. Since I was leaving, I sold him my equipment and gave him the little business we had started, and we moved.

Life lesson...

I had no idea what I was doing in business. I had no business even starting a business, but I did it anyway. I figured it out along the way. NEVER let your lack of experience, education, or training stop you from doing want you want to do, and NEVER listen to well-intentioned people who tell you that you can't do something!! Your future is in your hands, not theirs.

CHAPTER 16

ROUND TWO

"Never give up on a dream just because of the time it will take to accomplish it. The time will pass anyway."
~Earl Nightingale

Once again, we went to Georgia with no money, and I had no job.

Anita's father had to co-sign for a Pontiac Firebird for us. It was super nice. Anita had gotten a job as an assistant manager at an apartment complex, and part of her salary was a free one-bedroom apartment. This time at least when we showed up, we had a place to live.

On the drive down to Georgia, the engine in our new car started having problems. It was burning a quart of oil every 100 miles. When we finally arrived at our new apartment, and I pulled into the parking space and turned the car off, the engine seized up. It never started again. The engine was blown. Our car was shot, and we hadn't even made the first payment on it. Now what?

Fortunately, Anita could walk from our apartment over to the office, so that was not a problem. I, however, needed a car and a job. We were down to our last $200 in cash.

After looking through the paper, I found a car that was listed for $200. We got a ride over to see it. I offered the guy $190 because I needed the other $10 for gas to get home. He took it, and we were off. As soon as I drove away, it started raining. I turned on the windshield wipers, and I kid you not, they flew off the car. The car only had high beams, no low beams. None of the gauges on the dashboard worked, including the speedometer or the gas gauge. I had to stick a coat hanger in the gas tank to see if it was wet so I would know how much gas was in the car. Whenever it rained, or I was driving at night, I had to stick my head out the window to see the road. I used to bring a cup of hot water with me in the morning in the winter and pour it on the windshield to melt the frost. This was my reality. I was really something back then.

Our apartment literally had no furniture, not even a bed; we slept on the floor. We ate dinner sitting on the floor in an empty dining room and listened to a little Time Life transistor radio because that was all we had.

I applied for a job with a construction company and lied on the application, telling them that I had a college degree. The company hired me. This was in January of 1988. I made $400 a week. Truthfully, in "1988 dollars," I thought I was rich. After my first paycheck, we bought an air mattress to sleep on. After my second paycheck, we bought a TV. After a month of working, we got a real mattress and a box spring that we bought out of some guy's storage unit. We were almost normal!

Six or seven months passed, and we had furniture and another used crappy car. It wasn't much, but it was progress.

Part of my job for the construction company was doing payroll on Monday nights. The company I worked for would not let me start doing payroll until I was done with my workday at 7 PM.

"On a typical Monday night, I would be there until 2 AM doing invoices and writing checks; then, I had to be back at work the next morning at 7 AM."

I was doing payroll one night at about midnight with my wife sitting with me to keep me company. I have to say she really supported me in anything I did. She was good about that. I remember being dead tired and writing out a check to the landscaper for $14,000 for that week.

Now, this guy was a George Michael wannabe. He had the beard, hair, and clothes. Every time I saw him, I laughed. Except for this night, I couldn't laugh, as I sat there in the unfinished, unheated basement of that house, writing him a check for $14,000 while he was home asleep in bed.

That light bulb came back. I turned to my wife and said, "Oh my God. Once again, **one of us is stupid**." Like I said before, I knew which one it was.

Within a couple of weeks, I quit that job and started another landscaping business. Like the last time, I bought a mower, weed eater, blower, a ream of paper, and some markers. We were off once more, driving through subdivisions and sticking flyers in mailboxes. This was round two.

And here is the lesson...

Be ready for the light bulb...and when it turns on; don't ignore it!

CHAPTER 17

I HATED EVERY DAY

"Letting go doesn't mean giving up, but rather accepting that there are things that cannot be."
~Unknown

To this day, I cringe when I pass a landscaping crew.

My friends will remind me when I'm having a bad day... "Hey, Brian, it's better than landscaping."

I was miserable every day for ten years. I hated what I was doing. I was under tremendous stress, and I took it out on my family. Every failure was another hit to my self-image. Every time I couldn't pay the bills or could not take care of my wife and children financially, I was reminded that I was not the success that I wanted to be. The more stress I was under, the more I cracked the lid on that anger box and let it out.

I was demanding. Everything had to be done my way. There was no discussion, and I took no input. I valued nobody's opinion. I was an idiot. If you deviated, or even questioned my decision making, I would let you know how I felt about it. I was "always right." Unfortunately for me, looking back, I was probably more like "rarely right." The problem was stress. It was the overhead, the employees, the payroll, and the complaining customers. All of it was too much. Let's not forget I had NO IDEA what I was doing and that I was making it up as I went along. I was the stereotypical small businessperson that I see so much of today. They are exactly like me back then, with no clue and no experience.

I have had so many conversations with people who are managers for big companies who have told me they are going to go out and start a business with all of the knowledge and experience they have gained running a division for another company. We generally get into a discussion about what it takes to be successful in business, and they usually tell me about how they ran a huge budget and had lots of people working for them. This leads them to believe that they know how to run their own company. My response is always the same. "If you have never laid awake on Thursday night because you couldn't cover payroll Friday afternoon, you have no idea how to run a small business... If it's not your money you're spending, then you have no idea what you're doing in your own business." Of course, none of them believe me, and most of them go on to fail and lose a small fortune. You cannot bring a big company mentality into a bootstrapping environment. It just doesn't work.

"In my case, it wasn't just the business that I struggled with; it was my inner struggle around my success and failures that compounded the issues that I struggled with as well."

Every failure (and there were a lot of them) was another devastating blow to my ego and the competition I had going in my head with all the nameless and faceless people who were better than me and judging me. That is a lot of pressure to put on yourself, and it was not healthy.

Despite my inner struggles, we achieved a little bit of success in 1995 and 1996. We lived in a home that we liked and had two other rental properties. I drove a Mercedes and had a sports car, a motorcycle, and a Jeep. I also had a new daughter, Stephanie. By this time, she was about two years old.

One of the many challenges I had was my definition of success. Remember, I was the kid who was going to get everything that other people had and that I wanted. I needed to look successful, and that meant I needed to have a lot of things. I also didn't actually own any of my properties. The bank owned them, and I had to make payments. There is a life lesson coming up here shortly. But as far as I was concerned, I was on a roll since I had a bunch of stuff. That meant I was successful.

I was actually starting to believe I had begun to make it.

Then somewhere around the end of 1996, the wheels started coming off the bus at my landscaping company.

I had seven offices at the time and over forty employees, but was completely dependent on the income from my business to pay my bills. And I had no savings.

Like a lot of people in this country, I looked good, so people thought I was successful, but I was living paycheck to paycheck even though I owned the company.

At the time, I did not have a credit account with my suppliers. We were doing a lot of work on commercial projects, and I was writing my largest supplier a check every time I needed something. They would hold it until the end of the month when I got paid and then deposit all my checks. We were writing checks to our suppliers for about $150,000 a month. At some point near the end of 1996, our largest account fired us.

In our world, when you got fired, your client(s) also held your last pay for 3-4 months with threats of lawsuits, lawyers, legal fees, and dragging out paying you for years.

When my company was fired, in one 30-day period, I went from looking good to being in serious trouble. I did not get paid that month, but my vendors deposited the checks. Now, remember I was living paycheck to paycheck and had zero savings and no money in my checking account. It was devastating.

I bounced 130 checks at the bank at $32 apiece. Not only could I not cover the checks, but I now had over $4000 in bounced check fees that I could not pay for. The bank closed my account, told me I was not welcome there anymore and threatened me with a lawsuit for the money.

My vendors also all started coming after me for their money. I could not blame any of these people; it was all my fault. I lost everything. In a short period of time, I sold everything at fire-sale prices, including the houses, cars, and furniture. We were living in an empty house with an infant while I was waiting on the sale of it to close. That's when my mother came to visit, felt sorry for me, and bought me new furniture. After she left, I sold it. She came back to visit a couple of months later and asked,

"Where's the furniture?" I said, "Mom, I had to eat and feed my daughter... I sold it."

My electric was turned off two days before Christmas because I could not pay the bill. On New Year's Eve in 1996, my car was repossessed. By the end of January 1997, I owned nothing, and I had nothing. After selling everything I had and paying off the people that I owed, I was left with $5000, a wife, a three-year-old, and no place to live.

Once again, I was a failure. I took the $5000 and convinced a man to lease-purchase me his house with $5000 down. Then I moved my family in and started doing small landscaping jobs by myself again.

I was depressed.

Life lesson...

Do NOT live above your means. If you don't have the money to pay for what you want or the money in savings to back it up, don't buy it. The stress of being broke with a lot of possessions is not a good feeling. Don't do it.

As a side note, I started another company, and eighteen months later, sold it for $1 million in stock and cash. This next company took me down a completely different path that set the stage for the lifestyle I have today. If my landscaping company had not failed—which was devastating to me at the time—I would not be where I am now.

CHAPTER 18

NEGATIVE TO POSITIVE

"Whatever you get from being negative,
I hope it's enough. Because it's costing you plenty."
~Michael Hyatt

It was the beginning of 1997.

My business had failed.

I was broke and depressed, yet still had a family to feed.

I had let my health insurance lapse because I could not make the payments. But like a lot of people in this country, I figured nothing bad was going to happen if we didn't have insurance. I was wrong.

We had taken my daughter in for a check-up with her pediatrician. While in the appointment, the pediatrician said, "I don't want you to worry, but I want you to go see a cardiologist."

**"When we saw the cardiologist, he said,
'I don't want you to worry, but I want your
daughter to have an echocardiogram.'"**

Two doctors had said not to worry, but they were now running my daughter through testing for her heart. I was worried.

After the echocardiogram was complete, we got the news. Stephanie had an atrial septal defect. She had a large hole in the side of her heart that would require open-heart surgery, and we had no insurance. The doctor told us we could wait probably another year or so until she was four or five to have the surgery; fortunately, we got lucky and managed to get Blue Cross to cover her with a two-year waiting period. If they hadn't done that, I have no idea what we would have done.

However...

I must tell you at this point that there will be an underlying theme in this book about negative turning into positive. All the failures that I thought were setbacks at the time they happened were actually building blocks in my life. As I reflect on my life now, I can see a pattern. In each and every case, the negative that I thought was so devastating ended up being positive in the future. The question is...*did all those negatives turn into a positive because of fate or some greater plan? Was it God, or did I make the positive happen? Was I in control or not??* We will get back to this theme later...but for now...let's return to the story about Stephanie.

In our case, the two-year wait turned out to be A HUGE blessing for my daughter. As the two-year deadline approached, I had switched careers and was selling insurance.

My daughter's cardiologist planned to perform the open-heart surgery by opening her up from her neck to her belly button. It's hard to even imagine doing that to a four-year-old. And then she would live with the scars forever.

Think about a 16-year-old girl on the beach with those types of scars. It would be tough. We were really struggling with what this procedure would do.

Then thirty days before her surgery, I was on an appointment trying to sell an insurance policy to a woman in her home. She was a nice old lady, but she was too old to buy my policy. It felt like a total waste of my time. Not wanting to be rude, I sat and talked to her for a bit. I told her about my daughter and the upcoming surgery. She then asked me if I had ever heard of Dr. Banks at the Miami Children's Hospital. That was a strange question, and a little taken aback, I said no. She replied that I should look him up because he could help me with my daughter. I thanked her and told her I would, then left.

When I got home, I looked him up and was amazed. As it turns out, he was a pioneer in arthroscopic surgery specifically designed for Stephanie's issue. He could go in with a camera and correct the issue with only a 2-inch scar. He had just started performing the surgery in the past year and had done over 300 of them at the time. I immediately called his office and asked about the surgery. His office asked me to send Stephanie's records to them and not to schedule the surgery with her other doctor until they called me back. We sent Stephanie's records to his office and waited. A few days later, they called and said Stephanie was an excellent candidate, and Dr. Banks would do the surgery. We were excited. However, we had to get to Miami in two weeks and were still broke at the time. So, we weren't sure how we were going to get her there. I ended up meeting another client that same week who, after hearing my story about my daughter, told me about an organization called Angel Flights.

Angel Flights

Angel Flights is a volunteer pilot association that flies children with critical medical issues and their parents who cannot afford to travel to hospitals around the country for free. They flew my family back and forth to Miami and did not charge us. Years later, when I became a pilot, I flew Angel Flights missions. I have flown a lot of missions for them over the years. It is my small way of giving back. Every time somebody thanks me for flying them somewhere, I tell them the story of my daughter. I was in their shoes once, and I am happy to do it.

Two weeks later, my daughter's surgery was a success. Today she has a small 2-inch scar instead of a scar from her neck to her belly button. She is excited about life.

Remember, the only reason she could take advantage of this opportunity to have this new and minimally invasive surgery was that I had lost my insurance…because I could not pay for it…because my business had failed.

During that two-year waiting period, Dr. Banks pioneered this new procedure and performed it on 300 patients just in time for Stephanie to need it. If I had not lost my insurance, or my business had not failed, I would not have waited two years for her to have the surgery. If I had not waited, Stephanie would have a scar all the way down the front of her body. My business failing and not being able to pay for my insurance seemed like a devastating blow when faced with her medical issue. I stressed about this for two years. In the end, it turned out to be the best thing that could've happened. My business failure saved my daughter from a life of issues with terrible scars. I have no idea who that old lady was, and I never spoke to her again. I'm sure, by now, she has passed away, but if I could see her today, I would thank her. She made a difference in my and my daughter's life, and she never knew it.

That pattern of negative turning to positive has happened so many times in my life that I almost never get upset anymore when something bad happens. Many times, it has been years down the road before I figured out the positive that came from the negative. But it has happened every time. This includes my eventual divorce. I have not yet realized the entire positive outcome, although I have realized some of it... But that story comes later.

Life Lesson...

Sometimes things need to fall apart so they can get better. Not every bad situation is actually bad. It may actually be really good, but you just can't see it yet. So don't get too excited when you think something bad has happened. Don't stress yourself out and cause unneeded problems. The better thing might be right around the corner.

CHAPTER 19

GROUNDHOG DAY

"To carry adequate life insurance is a moral obligation incumbent upon the great majority of citizens."
~Franklin D. Roosevelt

At the beginning of 1997, I was back where I started ten years earlier, doing landscaping by myself with one guy that was my helper.

I was not happy.

A friend of mine had started selling health insurance at the beginning of the year. He came to see me one day trying to sell me some insurance and told me that I should start selling insurance with him. My response was, "I have sold used cars, and I have sold Amway. I am not going to sell insurance."

> **"One of the reasons that I didn't want to sell insurance was that I couldn't stop thinking about the movie *Groundhog Day*."**

In the movie, Bill Murray's character runs into Needle Nose Ned every day. Needle Nose Ned was the insurance guy. Ned had a briefcase, trench coat, and his funny insurance guy hat. Murray's character can't get away from him fast enough and, in one scene, punches him in the face. This was my perception of an insurance salesman, and I wanted no part of it. My friend, Sonny, however, kept coming back.

For four months, every time he would see me, he would pull out a copy of a big check he had just gotten and show me. Every check was bigger than the last one I saw. He would then say something like, "Look how much money I am making doing this."

Remember, I was miserable. I was a failure. I had lost everything and was back to landscaping on my own and living in a house with no furniture again. So after four months of seeing these bigger and bigger checks, I finally gave in and agreed to try it.

I asked him how I could get started. He said, "Give me a check for $500 for twenty leads. I will take you on one sales call, and then you're on your own." I gave him a check and went on the sales call. He made the sale while I sat there and watched. When we got in the car, he told me he had just made $400 in commission. I was amazed. It seemed pretty easy to me, too. So I said, "Let's do it," and was off to the races.

I sold insurance at night after landscaping all day, making prospect calls on Monday and Tuesday and setting appointments for Wednesday through Saturday. At the end of the first week, I walked into the insurance office and handed my boss a stack of twelve applications. He looked at the stack, then at me, and said, "How many is that?" I said, "Twelve." He then asked me how many leads I'd bought, and I said, "Twenty." After pausing for a second, he said, "Let's go to lunch." At lunch that day, he told me that I was probably in the top two percent of sales performances for the company nationwide. He wanted to know how I did it, and was it just a fluke. I told him that people called about insurance, and I sold it to them. I explained that I didn't know if it was a fluke, but that we would figure that out over the next several weeks.

I made more money part-time at night selling health insurance than I did all day landscaping.

My sales trend continued for the next couple of months. After the first sixty days, I was the top agent in the office. After ninety days, I was responsible for nearly fifty percent of all sales for the agency that had around ten agents. Like I said earlier, "Who knew...I could sell?!"

Life lesson here...

You may have talents that you haven't discovered yet. These talents may lead you to bigger and better things. Don't be afraid to try something new, and don't be afraid of failing. You might find out you have an amazing future that you've never even thought about.

CHAPTER 20

I QUIT

"Don't say maybe if you want to say no." ~Paulo Coelho

So there we were, deep into 1997.

I was still landscaping during the day and selling insurance at night. By this time, the money from my part-time insurance sales had surpassed my full-time landscaping income. But I was tired of doing both, and something had to give.

One Saturday morning, I had three landscaping appointments to do bids for jobs. I went to the first appointment and was standing in someone's backyard doing an estimate. The homeowner was talking to me about something, but I was completely disconnected from the conversation. His lips were moving, but I had no idea what he was saying.

I stood there thinking I hate this, and I don't want to do it anymore.

Right in the middle of him talking to me, I just closed my workbook, told him that I would get back with him, and then I got in my truck and drove away. I called Anita and told her that I quit. She said, "You quit what?" I told her that I was going to quit landscaping and that I would never do it again, ever, I was done. Her response was: "You can't quit. We have to pay the bills!" I told her we would find another way and that this new insurance business was going to work. I then called Joe, the guy who worked for me in landscaping, and told him if he wanted to be in business for himself, he had two more appointments that day he needed to go to because I was done. His response was also, "What?!!!" And then, "Did I just lose my job??" I said, "No... You have been promoted to owner. Now get out there. Customers are waiting for you!!"

I never went back to landscaping again. To this day, I will not cut grass, dig holes, or do virtually anything in my yard. I just won't do it.

A couple of weeks later, Anita and I went to a restaurant. I was beat up and slumped down in my chair with my hands in the pockets of my leather jacket. My landscaping company had failed. I'd started it over, and then I'd quit to sell insurance. I had absolutely no idea what I was doing. So, I told her that night, "This has to work. It has to because if it doesn't, I don't know what I will do. I'm out of options, and I'm too tired to try anything else." As we sat there picking at our food, I just kept saying, "This has to work..."

Life lesson...

You can't keep on doing something that doesn't make you happy. Life is short. The older you get, the faster it moves. If you're not happy, change what makes you unhappy. Find a better way. Do something different. Don't be rash about it, but figure it out before it's too late.

CHAPTER 21

BIG MISTAKE...BIG...HUGE

"Nothing is more expensive than a missed opportunity." ~H. Jackson Brown, Jr.

After the first sixty days of selling insurance for the agency I was working under, my sales levels and close rates had gotten so high that the agency forwarded their Yellow Pages' phone number to my home phone. I was by far the number one agent at the company. Once I started getting those calls, my production went through the roof. I was killing it in sales from that ad. My new career field was rolling along. What I was doing was working.

One weekend in September, I was up in Tennessee, visiting my mother in Knoxville. I pulled out a Yellow Pages book, took a look in the insurance section, and noticed that there were no big ads for selling health insurance. I called the local rep for the Yellow Pages in Knoxville that day and bought a quarter-page ad in the next book that was coming out December first. I did this because the deadline for the annual publishing was the next week, and I needed to make a decision. I had not talked to the agency I worked for yet, but I was confident that with my track record, this was a no-brainer decision.

When I got back to Atlanta, I visited the guy who owned the agency I worked for. I told him that I wanted to expand the agency into different states and explained that I would take all the risk and spend all the money upfront, but I wanted him to pay me a higher percentage based on my sales. The insurance world is a little bit like multilevel marketing. The owner was making thirty percent of everything I sold. The guy who brought me in was making twenty percent, and I was making sixteen percent. I asked the owner to raise me up to twenty percent with the contingency that I would expand his business and increase his sales—which would result in everyone making more money. I was shocked when he said no.

"I love this line from a movie you probably know, 'You work on commission, right? Big mistake...big... Huge.'"

I owned a purple Dodge Stratus at the time. It was the only car I could get after my landscaping company went under and with my bad credit. I got it at one of those "buy here, pay here" car lots. I also had a bag phone (aka a car phone in a bag) in the car with me. After my conversation with the owner, I left and was driving to an appointment to sell an insurance policy. I picked up the phone and called the insurance carrier that we represented. I told them I wanted to go out on my own and that they should give me a contract directly. Once again, I was shocked when they said no. As you know by now, I am not very fond of people telling me no. It's almost a challenge. They told me they could not give me a contract since I worked underneath one of their existing agencies. The owner of the agency had a lock on my sales production.

I hung up the phone and continued driving to my appointment. After about five minutes, one of those light bulb epiphany moments hit me. I called the guy at the insurance company back and asked him a different question. "If you cannot give me a contract," I asked, "Will you give one to my wife?" The man asked if she was a licensed agent. I said, "She will be in thirty days." He told me in that case, in thirty days, he would give her a twenty-five percent contract. That was five points higher than what I'd asked for at the agency I was currently working for! But she would have to be the face and name of our new company. I told him that was perfect and that I would get back to him as soon as she had a license. My next call was to my very pregnant wife. The conversation went something like this..."Honey, I know you're like eight months pregnant, but you need to go get your insurance license immediately. We are going into business for ourselves!!" I cannot remember her exact response, but it was something along the lines of "&$@;?$&@$)&!"

Thirty days later, on December first, my wife had an insurance license, and our first agency called Georgia Health and Life was born.

Here is the life lesson...

It's a repeat, but worth repeating. If the world tells you no, try a different path. If it tells you no again, try another path. If you want it badly enough, keep trying different paths until you get a yes. You do not have to accept a "no," and you do not have to give up because somebody else tells you to. You are in control of whether or not you succeed or fail.

CHAPTER 22

AMBITIOUSLY LAZY

"I always choose a lazy person to do a difficult job because he will find an easy way to do it." ~Bill Gates

What are the two primary motivators that drive ninety percent of salespeople?

The first one is easy.

It's what most people think is the only thing that motivates them. They are motivated by money. That one is obvious.

The second one is a little trickier, and very few people know it. Understanding it, however, is the key to running a successful sales organization. We will get into more of the consequences of this motivator in the next book. For now, let's talk high level. Salespeople are also motivated by laziness.

I understand the second answer seems to contradict the first answer.

Let me explain.

I have trained and managed hundreds if not thousands of salespeople in the last twenty years.

Anyone who has ever managed a group, or organization of salespeople, should understand what I'm telling you, although they may not have recognized the truth before reading it here.

Salespeople will work very hard until they hit their personal quota. Once they hit it, their work ethic drops off, and then they become lazy and go on cruise control until the next sales period.

In a normal week or month, that quota is whatever amount of money they need, or want, to make to maintain their lifestyle, or to achieve a goal. The quota is different for everybody. Sometimes you will see a steady producer put in more work than normal because they have a bill coming up, or something they want. Once they achieve that goal, however, they tend to fall right back into their normal pattern. Salespeople will rarely ever produce more than their own personal self-worth, or self-image *thinks* they are capable of producing. This is why sales organizations have contests all the time. They are used to crank up the production level to give salespeople something special to achieve. This is why some organizations encourage their salespeople to get into debt. Debt is a motivator. The worst type of salesperson is the one who doesn't need money.

I have always considered myself to be ambitious, but I also know that I am lazy. The trick to being successful in sales is combining the two elements to create a system that allows you to grow while also keeping you from doing all the work...or any of it, if at all possible. I will work really hard so that I don't have to work at all later. I call this ambitiously lazy.

Georgia Health and Life was now up and running. My wife had gotten her insurance license. I had quit the agency I worked for, and we set up shop. She was the principal agent, although I did all the work. At this time, I was working out of my back bedroom at the house. This was super convenient except that we had just had our second child. The house was not very big, and it was difficult sometimes taking sales calls with the baby screaming in the background. And my son Michael was certainly a screamer.

I had Yellow Pages ads now in Atlanta, Georgia, and Knoxville, Tennessee. Here was the problem. Yellow Pages ads work. The phone rang off the hook. People wanted to buy. That was both good and bad news.

The problem was after I talked to the people who called from the ads, I actually had to go see them personally to do the application. So, I took calls during the first part of the week for Knoxville and set up appointments on Thursdays and Fridays. I would then drive three hours on Thursday to Knoxville, go on appointments on Thursday afternoon and Friday morning and then drive back to Atlanta Friday night. During the rest of the week, I would take calls in Georgia and run to appointments all over the city.

Another problem was that when I was on appointments, nobody was answering the phone. As most people know, when you call a company, and they do not answer, you generally hang up and call somebody else. I was losing money because I was not home to answer the phone. I lost a lot of revenue on marketing dollars I had already spent. And even though I recognized the problem, I was not sure how to fix it. Insurance applications back then required a physical signature and a physical check.

Over the course of my first several months running these Yellow Pages ads, I had learned that I could do most of the selling over the phone. That was the easy part for me. The appointment with the client ended up being nothing more than filling out an application and getting a check. That was another easy part, although it was the most time-consuming. My dilemma was, *how do I keep answering the phone and selling and still go on appointments?* So, I hired a guy named Arron, who was a licensed insurance agent. He was allowed to fill out the applications. Aaron's job was to drive around to the appointments I set for him and fill out applications for me, so I could do the selling on the phone.

"This was a perfect system. I no longer missed calls and more than made up enough money to pay Arron from the increased business. I never had to leave the house. This business model was a winner."

I then decided to expand to another city. We took out an ad in Chattanooga, Tennessee. It was on the way to Knoxville, so that worked out well. This expansion, however, created a whole new problem. I now had more calls coming in than I could handle—it was the same problem. I would be on the phone with one client when another client would call in. But I couldn't answer the phone again, so the people would hang up and call someone else. I was losing money once more. I even hired my mother at this point to help run appointments in Knoxville, where she lived. Unfortunately, that didn't work out as I had hoped, and I had to fire her. Talk about awkward... How many people have fired their mother?!

This new arrangement also began to create a problem with my wife. I was complaining because the baby was too loud and because people were walking all over our house while she had a new infant. I had no choice but to move the business out of the house. My first office was three miles up the road.

Our business was rolling along pretty good, but I was getting bored. So I got to thinking, If I could just get rid of Arron and still get those applications filled out, I could make even more money.

It was 1998. Faxed documents were in the beginning stages of being considered legal. I approached my insurance carrier and asked them if I could start submitting faxed documents instead of originals. This had never been done before. After some legal wrangling, they agreed to test it with my agency. We would sell health insurance over the phone, collect a faxed signature, and a faxed copy of the check and submit it to the carrier via fax.

We gave it a whirl and wound up creating the first health insurance call center in America. In addition, we made Arron an inside agent instead of a courier. He was now producing revenue instead of costing the company money. Even better!!!

A year after we started Georgia Health and Life, we were expanding quickly. We now had Yellow Pages ads in six states and thirteen cities. We had five agents and a small administrative staff. By 1999, we had created the largest individual health insurance agency in America for the carrier that we worked for. We were competing against field agencies with hundreds of sales-people—and we had five. The difference was we had a better, more efficient way of doing business.

Side note...

Remember the guy who told me I could not expand his agency? If he had just given me the extra four points I had asked for, I would've built that entire business for him! He lost potentially millions of dollars by being greedy. This new system of sales was born out of me being lazy. I wanted more, but I didn't want to work harder. So, I created systems to do the work more efficiently.

And here are two lessons...

1. *Don't be greedy, and never underestimate the guy who's working for you. He might just be the next big thing. That guy who wouldn't give me the four points was out of the insurance business a couple of years later. I have no idea what happened to him, but he missed out on millions of dollars.*

2. *There will always be a better way to do something. Either you will figure it out or someone else will.*

CHAPTER 23

I SOLD MY FIRST COMPANY

"The gap between what's expected and what you deliver
is where the magic happens, in business and in life."
~Jay Baer

In the fall of 1999, the dot com boom was in full swing. Everybody was making millions of dollars with these stock option things I kept hearing about. My insurance agency was humming along, and I was not really working that hard, so I decided that I should let the agency run itself. Instead, I would work for one of these internet companies. I wanted to get me some of those options and become a dot com millionaire.

I found an internet insurance startup based in Atlanta called Simplyhealth.com. They had raised $27 million of venture capital. The CEO was twenty-seven years old. They were advertising for a director of sales position. I applied for it even though they wanted someone with a degree and preferably an MBA. The truth is I didn't technically apply because I didn't have the qualifications, or a resume. I had only been in the insurance business for two years. Prior to that, as you know, I ran a failed landscaping company. I did not think that was the type of resume this company was looking for. So instead of sending them a formal resume, I sent an email telling them I was interested in the position. It was a long shot, but I had nothing to lose.

To my surprise, I got a call back from a guy named Dan. Dan asked me about my background and my current company. He asked what I was going to do with my company if they hired me. I told him it could run on autopilot and that I would leave it alone and come work for them. He told me that would be a conflict of interest, and said, "We will probably want to buy your company as well as hire you." I was a bit stunned. I had not considered selling my company as I didn't really understand that it had value. This was my first experience in selling a company and my first experience with someone telling me that what I had built was worth a lot of money. I would even go so far as to say this was the first time someone else in the world had told me that I was successful, and they wanted what I had. It was a pretty amazing feeling for me at the time.

Three years earlier, I had lost my landscaping company and everything I owned. My car had been repossessed, and I couldn't open a checking account because I'd bounced so many checks. My credit was shot. Two and a half years after I started in the insurance business having absolutely no idea what I was doing and six weeks after I'd decided I wanted to have some of those stock option things, Georgia Health and Life was acquired in a seven-figure cash and stock deal. It was crazy.

Life lesson...

Yes, my whole world fell apart when the landscaping company crashed and burned. What I didn't know was that two and a half years later, I would be worth $1 million on paper. You have no idea what's around the next corner. So, just relax and wait for it. The truth is the only thing I'd lost was a landscaping company that made me unhappy every day. Once again, something that was bad at the moment became something much, much better. If my landscaping company had not failed so spectacularly, I would probably still be doing it and still be unhappy. That's a scary thought.

CHAPTER 24

MCDONALD'S SAFETY NET

"If 'Plan A' didn't work, the alphabet has twenty-five more letters. Stay cool." ~Claire Cook

A few years back, during my landscaping days, I met a man who taught me a lesson that I have carried with me and that I actually applied when we sold Georgia Health and Life.

I was out on a landscaping bid in a swanky neighborhood in north Atlanta. I remember going to the front door and ringing the bell for my appointment, and nobody answered. I hated it when people set up appointments, and then they were not home. So, I walked around the house looking for someone. When I got to the back of the house, I saw several people inside looking at carpet samples. I knocked on the back door to get their attention. Immediately this guy walked out the back door carrying a carpet sample. He asked me what I needed. I assumed he was the carpet salesman, and I told him I was there to see the owner to do an estimate for his landscaping, and I asked if the owner was home.

The guy informed me that he was the homeowner and had called me. I apologized for my mistake. After he told me what he wanted done for his landscaping, I went back out to my truck to write up an estimate. The guy who worked for me at the time looked over at the estimate and recognized the homeowner's name. He asked me if I knew him. I said no. He then proceeded to tell me that this was the newest member of the Atlanta Braves. He had just moved here from another state and team. When I heard that, I felt even worse for thinking he was a carpet sales-man. When I went back up to the house to give the guy his esti-mate, I apologized once again and explained that I was not a huge baseball fan. I told him, honestly, I did not know who he was. He actually thought that was humorous and said he preferred it that way.

I got the job that day and started taking care of his house for him. As time went on, I got to know him a little better.

I remember asking him one day why so many professional athletes ended up broke. He told me that too many of these guys become instant millionaires and suddenly think they are going to become instant billionaires. Somehow they think that their athletic skill translates into financial genius. They make horrible investments, get suckered by everybody in the world, and end up losing all of their money.

He told me that he paid cash for everything he had, and he kept his money in T-bills. He did not make a lot of interest, but he knew exactly where his money was. If his career ended and he could no longer earn an income, he knew that he was safe for the rest of his life because he had a safety net. I loved that concept.

> **"In January of 2000, I closed on the sale of Georgia Health and Life. I paid off all of my debt, and after taxes had enough money left over to pay off my house."**

I remember going down to the bank to meet with the mortgage guy and telling him that I wanted to pay off the house. He told me I was crazy and that I should invest my money in the stock market as it was skyrocketing. In return, I told him the story about my client and that I would much rather secure my house than take a risk on the market. This banker literally spent twenty minutes trying to convince me to invest my money in tech and internet stocks. I told him, "No, I don't want to do that. Please pay off my house." I figured with my house paid for and no debt, if I lost all my income, I could work at McDonald's and still maintain my lifestyle. I called this my McDonald's Safety net.

In March of 2000...ninety days later, the internet bubble burst, and the stock market crashed. If I had invested that money, I would've lost almost all of it. My McDonalds Safety Net was in full swing.

And here is the lesson...

Protect your future. If you know what you're doing is the right thing, do not let somebody else talk you out of it. Do what you know is right.

Side note...

This particular lesson served me well when in 2006, we sold a MUCH bigger company. A couple of my partners, unfortunately, did not learn this lesson. They went bankrupt after getting anywhere from $6 million to $15 million in cash. But we will get to that later.

CHAPTER 25

YOU'RE NOT QUALIFIED TO RUN YOUR OWN BUSINESS

"Perhaps when you thought you weren't good enough, the truth was that you were overqualified."
~Unknown

The beginning of 2000 was very exciting for me.

I had sold my company.

I was out of debt and owned my house outright.

I was a paper dot com millionaire with a bunch of those stock options that were going to be worth millions in the future... I now had enough of them to wallpaper my kitchen... Which was about what they were worth.

The company that bought us moved our office and all of our employees down to the parent company office on the Georgia Tech campus. I was a dot-commer and felt super cool. I had a company phone, company pager, and a company computer. I thought I was rolling.

Prior to the move downtown, we were in an office building in Woodstock, Georgia, where I had a big corner office with a TV and cable television. Honestly, I watched TV most of the day and did very little work.

The day after being acquired, I showed up at the new company and was given a 2 x 3 cubicle in the middle of the cubicle aisle in a crammed office space. I was a bit put off and went to see my new boss to ask why I was jammed in a cubicle and not put in an office. I was told that they appreciated that I had built the company to where it was, but that I was no longer qualified to run it. I was being demoted to a sales manager title.

The main problem, they told me, was that I did not have a degree. Without a degree, I shouldn't even really be a manager, and they absolutely could not put me onto the executive management team. I was informed they were bringing in a sharp young MBA to replace me and that I would work for him. I was now relegated to a manager role sitting in a cubicle farm, working for somebody who had never built a business and had no insurance experience.

It took a fair amount of discipline to keep the lid from cracking open on my anger box. I kept telling myself they have paid me a lot of money. They are giving me a decent salary, and I have a bunch of options that someday I will be able to cash in.

Over the next six months, I witnessed some of the most unbelievably stupid decision making and absurd spending I have ever seen. I didn't have an MBA like everybody else, but I could clearly see that what this new company was doing made no sense. What we should have been doing was trying to sell health insurance to individuals who were primarily self-employed.

One of my favorite examples of what not to do came from a campaign we ran with Delta Airlines. Our head of marketing told me that we were paying someone around $100,000 to interview our CEO. That interview was going to be played in the first-class section on every Delta flight from the East Coast to the West Coast. She was so excited about all the exposure we were going to get.

I asked her three questions. "Who is the typical person sitting in first class on the coast to coast Delta flight?" She thought about it and told me that it was a businessman who probably works for a big fortune 500 company. In response, I asked, "Do they buy their own insurance?" She said no. I replied, "Then why are we losing money, showing them an interview of our CEO?" I told her this was an incredible waste of the company's money. Her next statement blew me away. She told me we were supposed to lose money. Our investors expected us to lose money. Making money was not our primary concern. We were branding.

I didn't even know what to say. Venture capital is a different animal, as I would learn later when I sold my next company. This woman was fired not too long after that. I understand burn rate. I understand that you have to spend money to build something. But spending stupid money and never building anything seems like a huge waste of time and money. Clearly, she and the rest of this management team of sharp young MBAs had never spent their own money and had no idea how to build a business. I could write a whole book on the crazy stories from that early dot com experience. But as I keep reminding you—you'll have to wait. I will tell those stories in another book.

About six months after I started working for this company, I came to the realization that we actually did have something valuable. It wasn't the retail call center that we were building; it was our software. Back in the year 2000, the internet was still young. Insurance companies were still reliant on individual salespeople out in the field selling their products. And those salespeople were using paper charts with pricing grids based on up to ten different factors to figure out pricing for their clients. If you wanted to give your client three or four options, you had to do the math process three or four times. It took time. After your salesperson got the pricing figured out, they then had to fill out the long paper application. When that was done, the application had to be mailed to the insurance carrier.

Our software platform, on the other hand, was pretty slick. You could put in the client's basic information, and it would give you a whole series of quotes from multiple carriers. You could see all the prices in one easy format, and with the click of a button, pull up the correct application to fill out. Today, this technology seems very simple, but back then, it was revolutionary. I sat down with the head of technology, a guy named Mike, and told him that I thought we should start selling our software to our insurance carrier partners. Mike thought it was a good idea and told me to write up a business plan. I went down to the office supply store and bought a software package to write a business plan. It took me about a month, but I wrote a business plan called Simply Health Technologies. The plan was to sell our software as a hosted service. We would charge the carrier upfront to build it and then charge them again for every quote run. I put myself in the business plan as director of sales for this division.

"I figured if I could sell insurance, I could sell software."

When the plan was done, I went to see the CEO with my fresh business plan in hand. We could launch a whole new division and generate millions of dollars in software revenue while creating a huge recurring income stream. I showed him examples of other companies that were doing what I was proposing. His response was, "This is not our business plan. I won't support it." However, he said, "If you would like to try and sell this to a carrier, go ahead." He would not give me a budget for staff and would not support me, but if I could sell it, to go ahead and do it. I'm sure he laughed when I left his office. I mean, *who was that uneducated guy thinking he can change the business model and sell software?* With the help of two more people in the company, we began calling insurance carriers to see if they would be interested. They were.

The very first presentation we did was for an insurance carrier up in Milwaukee, Wisconsin. After two days of presentations, they told us they would be interested in buying the platform from us. Our second and third presentations were out in California to two of the largest insurance carriers in the country. After the first presentation, the second carrier said they would be interested in buying the software from us. We were selling the software package for over $2 million. Suddenly we had nearly $4 million in potential orders for this software. This was way more money than we were generating on the retail insurance side. Now, everyone in the company was interested in getting involved. We had a winner.

We had a third appointment with another insurance carrier in California coming up soon. My immediate boss then came to me and said, "Thank you for getting us started, but I'm going to take over from here. You don't need to go with us on the next appointment. You're not really qualified to sell software."

I was not happy. Once again, it took a lot of discipline to keep the lid from cracking open on that anger box. So, I stayed in Atlanta. Halfway through their presentation to the carrier I was excluded from, I got a call from Mike. He was in a panic. They needed me to fly to California on the next flight and save the deal. The guy doing the presentation was falling all over himself, and it was a disaster. They rescheduled the meeting for the next day, and I flew to California that night and met with everyone the next day. I ran through the presentation, and we closed the deal. We were now sitting on $6 million worth of software contracts after just six weeks. By now, even the CEO was interested, and the board of directors had heard what we were doing as well.

My original deal and my business plan had called for me to make a very small percentage of commission for everything that we sold. Upon signing this contract, I should have made commissions of around $60,000. I was excited. Everyone in the company was excited. We had a new business model.

The board of directors called a meeting. My desk was right outside the board room. I remember all the executives filing in and the doors closing. They were in the meeting for about two hours. When the meeting adjourned, everyone came out, and I was called into the CEO's office. He talked to me about the new business model and the old business. Somewhere along the line, he had decided that the new business model was actually his idea. He told me the board of directors wanted to create a whole new company and start pursuing the business plan I wrote with both more money and resources. This was awesome.

Then he dropped the bomb on me. While they appreciated everything I had done and that it was a good start, I wasn't qualified to be the head of sales for the software division. They were going to bring in a sharp young MBA to run it, and they wanted me to go back and be a manager on the retail insurance side.

I was stunned.

I wrote the plan.

I launched the product.

I sold the first three contracts.

I bailed them out of the California deal because the existing team couldn't do it.

Now, I wasn't qualified to be involved any further. Once again, I was pushed aside because I did not have a college degree.

That one English class and the conversation with my professor about jumping through hoops and me getting mad and quitting college haunted me. I went back to my desk and was so angry I just sat there staring at my computer for about fifteen minutes. Life wasn't fair. How could they push me aside when the division would not exist without me?

Life lesson...

It wasn't mine. It was theirs. I was just an employee, and all the whining and complaining and talk about how life isn't fair didn't mean a thing. As long as you are working for somebody else, it is their ball and bat; it is their game. There's nothing you can do, so you need to get over it and move on.

I went back to my desk, put on my coat, took everything that was mine out of my desk, crammed it in my pockets, and walked out the door. Then I got in my car and drove home. About half-way home, I got a call from my immediate boss. She wanted to know where I was and why I was not sitting at my desk. I told her the whole thing was bullshit, and I wasn't going to stay and work for them, that I quit. She said, "Okay. Good luck!" and that was the last time I talked to her. She was fired not too long after that. The guy they hired to head up the sales division did not sell another software contract for over a year, and he got fired, too. The investors put in another $5 million, and they stumbled along for a few years before even the CEO was fired and replaced.

The story, however, had a happy ending. That company ended up acquiring another company in Wisconsin. I continued to evolve from 2000 all the way up until 2015. At the beginning of 2015, this company went public. Shortly after that, they called me because they heard I was starting another company and told me they were interested in investing in and eventually buying my new company. It was round two... *Here we go again...*but I will tell that story in my next book.

CHAPTER 26

PIZZA

"Did you hear about the guy who took a second job as a pizza chef? He kneaded the dough!" ~Old dad joke

It was January 2001.

I'd just quit my six-figure job and had no income again.

Fortunately, I did have my McDonald's Safety Net in place.

Because I was out of debt, I did not need to make that much money. It was time to go back into business for myself.

One of my favorite things to do is go out to eat. I eat out 100 percent of the time unless somebody else is cooking. My food bill is one of the most expensive line items in my budget.

I'd always had fond memories of working at the pizza place in high school. It seemed like an easy business, so I figured *what the heck, why not open up a pizza restaurant?* Let me remind you that I don't cook…don't know how to cook…and have no desire to cook. I also had no idea how to run a restaurant. So naturally, I opened a restaurant and started cooking in what seemed to be a viable location…where a pizza place had closed.

Life lesson...

If a pizza place closes, don't open another pizza place in the same spot. IT WON'T WORK!!

Not knowing this life lesson, I opened my new restaurant and called it Grinder Pizza and Subs, with the idea that it would be my first of ten locations in the Atlanta market. It seemed logical to me that if you were going to have one, you should have ten. Always think big...

Unfortunately, about four or five months into this venture, I learned the life lesson I just told you about and came to realize that Grinders was not working. I did not want to be in the kitchen cooking. We were failing. I was miserable and wanted out.

Then one day, a guy walked into my restaurant and told me that he'd thought about buying the spot before I did. I was not about to tell him my newly learned life lesson, so instead, I told him he could buy the franchise that day if he liked. He told me that he did not have any money or any credit but that he was a great chef. "No problem," I told him. "I will owner finance it and will stay on the lease for the building. You can take over as soon as tomorrow. You don't even have to make any payments to me for three months while you build up your business."

It was an offer he could not refuse. He took over the pizza place, and I was out. It was June 2001.

Side note...

He failed, which is not surprising. This enforced my life lesson once again.

I eventually had to file a lawsuit against him.

"I was driving by the pizza place one night at about one in the morning when I noticed the door hanging open and the lights on. I pulled in to see what was going on. The new owner had come in after closing and gutted the place."

He took everything. He cut the pipes coming out of the walls and stole the sinks. He jacked the counters, ovens, and even the toilets. There was nothing left but an empty shell of the place, and he was gone. I never did get my money.

And here's the lesson.

If you have to finance something for somebody, chances are you're never going to get it. There is a reason they need you to finance it. It's usually because nobody else is dumb enough to give them financing. Second, if your business is failing, there's a pretty good chance the next guy is not going to be able to turn it around.

I am constantly amazed when I drive around and notice restaurant locations open and close every year under a new name and owner. It never ceases to astound me that people will sink their entire life savings into a closed restaurant. They think that the business will work if only they can get in there and run it.

There's a business tip in all of this: if the last three restaurants failed at a specific location, the next three are also going to fail. Save your money and don't invest in a restaurant there.

CHAPTER 27

LET'S DO IT AGAIN

"Ever tried. Ever failed. No matter. Try again.
Fail again. Fail better." ~Samuel Beckett

It was June 2001, and there I was again, unemployed with no income.

When I sold my insurance agency, I vowed I would not go back into the insurance business. The problem was I was pretty good at it, and it was pretty easy. I also didn't have anything else to do at the time, and as I stated earlier in the book, I had no education to fall back on or experience outside of landscaping and now insurance.

About this time, my friend Danny called me. This would not be the first time Danny called me about working together. I met Danny back in my landscaping days. He worked at a nursery where I bought a lot of my material. While he was there, he watched my landscaping company take off and then implode, and my world fall apart. He then watched me start my next company that I sold two and a half years later.

So, Danny called me one morning and said he wanted to quit working at the nursery and get into the insurance business. Also, he wanted me to teach him everything I knew. I thought about it, agreed to the plan, and then told him, "I'm going to start another agency, and you can come work for me." Just like that, we were back at my house sitting at the same desk and starting another company—two years after I'd sold the first one.

Like the first time I started, Danny sat on one side of the desk, and I sat on the other.

About a month into this new business, I was sitting in a restaurant, having a few cocktails with my wife. Honestly, I'd had a few too many at that point. While we were sitting there, I picked up the phone and called my friend Sonny who had gotten me into the insurance business originally.

Sonny had been running an agency for the past couple of years. I asked him if he would like to start a company together. The plan was that we would join our two agencies. He knew that I had recently sold my last one, and on the spot, we agreed to start a new partnership. We began the planning stages of our new company, adopted his company name, and launched Premier Financial Group.

We rented space and set everything up for the new business in a short period of time, then raised about $300,000 in working capital to start. We hired a new group of salespeople as well and scheduled them for training. It was our first day in business, September 11, 2001.

I was in the office doing a training class that morning for my new agents. We were all sitting around the giant conference room table when in the middle of my training, everyone's cell phones went off. The office phone started ringing off the hook, too. To be honest, I was a bit annoyed, but I continued my training for a little while. That didn't last long because my cell phone would not stop vibrating. When I looked down at it, I saw I had missed about five different calls.

I finally stopped the class, picked up my phone, and listened to my voicemails along with everyone else. The first plane had hit the tower in New York. All we knew was that it was a plane. Not knowing anything else, I assumed it was a small one. My voice messages were all the same: "Go watch TV." A few of us made phone calls, and we kept hearing the words "terrorist attack."

The news was unrelenting and terrifying, so I decided to stop the class, go to my house and watch TV to see what was going on. *Today is not the best day to start a new company*, I thought.

A bunch of people and I got to my house just in time to see the second plane hit the second tower. It was crazy. We sat there for the rest of the afternoon watching TV. Unfortunately, as they say, though, the show must go on. The bills would not stop coming, and people still expected me to pay them. So, the next morning we started again, and Premier Financial Group was off and running.

Over the course of the year, our new business expanded into three different offices. This turned out to be both a bad decision and the best decision I'd ever made. And there is a business lesson here… Keep your employees consolidated as long as possible.

Trying to manage multiple locations was a drain on time, resources, and money. Expansion made no sense at our size.

On the other hand, it did lead to a life-changing event for us.

Sometime in 2002, we decided to consolidate the offices. To do that, we had to break our lease at the main office. The company that owned our building was also located in the office park and was run by a guy named Seth. I tried to get ahold of Seth for months, but he was never around.

Finally, one day I walked into the building where I thought he might be and checked around to see if I could find him. Somebody stopped me and asked what I was doing and who I was. I told him that I was leasing the building next-door; we were expanding and needed to move. I needed to talk to somebody about my lease.

I then learned that Seth ran an internet marketing company. I had heard that they were making a lot of money. The guy who had stopped me in the hall asked me what I did, and I told him we sold health insurance online. After a brief conversation, he said, "You need to meet Seth!!"

Now, I had been trying to do that for two months. Then suddenly, I walk across the street to another building and into his office. That was the first time I met Seth, my future business partner, mentor, and a very great man.

Seth and I talked over the next couple of days about what he did and what I did and how we could do something together. Seth was positive, excited about life, and genuinely wanted to do something big.

"Seth's company had an online insurance product that they wanted to combine with my company."

After a few days of talking through it, we struck a deal. They would acquire my company and take care of all the marketing, and we would grow to ten times what we were then. We hugged it out. We were going to be huge. I went home that night very excited about the future. And then I went to work the next day.

When I went over to see Seth, a security guard met me at the door. I told him I was going to see Seth, and he told me Seth was no longer there. *What??!! He was the president of the company.*

I called Seth on his cell phone to find out what the hell had happened. He told me his partners and their lawyer had sued him and kicked him out of his own company. They accused him of stealing. I asked him how they could possibly do that. He told me they had accused him of doing business deals on the side without their knowledge. They were suing him, and he was now suing them. All of this had happened in less than fifteen hours from the last time I saw him. I asked him what I should do, and he told me his ex-partners would probably still do the deal with me, but he would not be a part of it.

I didn't like that.

Sure enough, later that day, I got a call from one of Seth's ex-partners, Jim. Jim told me they still wanted to do the deal. I remember I was driving down the road when Jim called me. He told me he was ready to sign with me. I thought about it for about ten seconds and then told Jim no, I was out.

I explained that I had made the deal with Seth and that I would not do the deal without him. Jim told me straight out: "Brian, this decision is going to change your life." I told Jim that might be the case, but I just could not bring myself to do the deal without Seth; he was my guy.

Jim hung up, and I never spoke to him again. Their online insurance product and that specific company were out of business within a year.

About the same time a year later, in March 2003, Seth settled his lawsuit with his ex-company. He had won, and they had to pay him and release his non-compete. By this time, I had consolidated our three offices into one larger office. Our company was moving along, but we were struggling a little bit with cash flow. Seth called me one day and said he wanted to talk. His lawsuit was over, and he wanted to go back into business together.

We went to lunch and talked about what we had been doing over the past year. Seth told me how much he appreciated that I had not done the deal without him. He was thankful for my loyalty and still wanted to do something together.

We decided that he would start another internet marketing company and would move into one of my back offices to get it started. He would also kick some money into the new company as well as my existing company. I would get equity in his company, and he would get equity in my company. Whichever company succeeded first would pay him back, and we would move on from there.

156

Seth brought in two other partners with him, and I had my partner Sonny, so there were a total of five of us as partners in this new company. Now, I knew Seth had made millions of dollars in his last company, and I had never done that, so I was pretty happy with our deal.

Life Lesson...

Money is not as important as loyalty. I could have made the easy decision to take the money, but instead decided to be loyal to my new friend. The first option would have had me out of business in a year. The second option made me over $10 million over the next three years

CHAPTER 28

CLOSE IT DOWN

"The doors we open and close each day decide the lives we live." ~Flora Whittemore

2003 rolled along.

My employees and I were selling insurance in the front of the office, and Seth and his four employees were running the new internet company in the back. Early on, Seth had decided to bring in another fifty percent partner on the new company. This partner was a big marketing agency based in Florida. They had invested about $65,000 in the server farm. So as it stood, they owned half of the internet company, and we owned the other half collectively as a group of five partners.

Things did not take off as we expected; we were not selling anything online and were paying salaries and expenses as well as running up debt that I was liable for in my company. As we approached the end of 2003, I knew the internet company had not done much business. But the insurance agency was rolling along and growing slowly.

Just after Christmas, my CPA, Don, came to see me. He shut my office door and said, "Brian, you need to close down the internet company." When I asked him why, he said we had burned through about $450,000 in cash, generated no revenue and that I was liable for all that money. Don said the company was draining the resources of the insurance agency and that if I didn't shut it down, it was going to bankrupt us. I was concerned. My faith in our new venture was gone.

The next morning I had a conversation with my wife about the whole situation and told her that I wanted out. It was not working; I owed a ton of money and was very discouraged and stressed. As usual, she told me that she supported me in whatever decision I made. I remember thinking, *quit being so damn accommodating and nice. Tell me I'm an idiot or something*!!! That was, of course, my old self-image problem rearing its ugly head.

At work, that day around lunchtime, Seth came into my office and sat down in the chair across from me. I can picture this conversation in my head today as if it happened five minutes ago. Seth was wearing a pair of ratty shorts, sneakers, and a T-shirt. He was the kind of guy who was worth probably $10 million but drove a pickup truck to work. You would never know he had money.

Seth informed me that our fifty percent partners had lost faith and wanted to be bought out. They were not happy that we were losing so much money and no longer believed in the company. It would take $66,000 of their investment to buy them out. I thought, *oh great. Now they want out. Why am I still in this thing?*

Seth told me that he would put up the money to buy them out and add it to our overall debt. The good news he said was that between the five of us, we would now own the entire company. I sat there and did the math in my head $450,000 + $66,000 *means I now owe $516,000.*

The conversation I'd had with my wife that morning echoed in my head. I still wanted out. Now our fifty percent partner also wanted out. I asked Seth if we should put more money into this thing...it was failing, after all. I shared the conversation I'd had with Don the previous day–that he had said we should shut it down. I was not sure spending another $66,000 was a good idea.

"Seth told me that the internet was like the lottery. Just keep throwing money at it, and when it eventually hits, it's a gusher."

He assured me that I needed to have vision. I remember saying, "Seth, we haven't made one single dollar... Not one dollar... Maybe this thing isn't going to work, and we really do owe a lot of money."

Seth shifted around in his chair and leaned forward. I could see he was getting a little frustrated with me. In reality, he had put up the $516,000. There was a hard look in his eyes as he said, "Brian, I'm going to make you a one-time offer. You give me my equity back. I will give you your equity back. You owe me nothing, and we walk away as friends."

The next two minutes changed my life, my children's lives, and my grandchildren's lives. I was about to make a generational decision.

I sat there staring at Seth, my mind racing. The conversation I'd had with my wife that morning and the knowledge that Seth had done this before and been successful was like a ping-pong ball going back and forth in my head.

At that moment, I could have gone either way. But my mind couldn't stop spinning. *Am I going to bet on me, or am I going to bet on the guy who's done this before?* Two minutes seemed like forever, and I'm pretty sure I was sweating. I wanted out, and there was my chance handed to me on a silver platter. After a huge internal struggle, I said, "Okay, Seth. **I'm in.**"

Side note...

I have a tattoo on my back shoulder that says, "I'm in." That conversation is where it came from.

It changed my life.

Seth looked at me and said, "Okay, good, but I don't ever want to have this conversation again." I agreed, and he got up and went back to work.

Seth bought out our fifty percent partner for $66,000 in December of 2003, and the five remaining partners then owned the entire company. Thirty days later, just like Seth had said a month earlier, we hit our first deal online. In 2004, that company did $6 million in revenue and made us $1 million in profit. Seth got all his money back, and we made a nice little profit for the partners. In 2005, we did $20 million in revenue and about $6 million in profit. I was forty years old, and that was the first year I'd personally made over $1 million in a single year. It was an amazing time in my life. I had started to achieve everything I had always wanted.

Shortly after that, I did what most people do who come into a lot of money, and I bought a couple of super-expensive cars and started building a giant house. Looking back, these were not great decisions, but the euphoria of new money is very hard to handle for most people, and I got caught up in it very easily.

In 2006, we did $35 million in revenue and $9 million in profit. I made $1.6 million that year.

Life was good.

Later that year, we accepted an offer to sell the company for $45 million in cash.

My family's life changed forever.

To this day, it still scares me when I think about how very close I was to making a different decision that day that Seth sat in my office and made me a one-time deal.

I think about the guys who sold us half of our company back for $66,000. They lost over $30 million dollars over the next two years.

Where would I be today if I had said no...?

As I sit here writing this book, my daughter just completed a trip around the world. She visited fourteen countries in four months. She has experienced things that very few people on planet earth have ever seen and done. There is no way she would have been able to have that experience if I had said no that day.

I might still be selling insurance and would have to live with the fact that I walked away from a deal of a lifetime.

Life lesson...

Sometimes you need to take the risk. Sometimes you need to bet on other people and not just yourself. Follow the track record.

Was it talent or luck? Why did I make those decisions? Why did I remain loyal to Seth when he was kicked out of his old company and sued? Why did I say yes instead of no when I really wanted out? Maybe it was both, but there's no way you can rule out the lucky part. I believe in luck.

Another side note...

If I had done the original deal with Seth's old company, and Seth would not have been sued by his partners, I would never have had the opportunity to partner with him on the new company.

Final side note...

If you come to my house, I have a beautiful bar and billiards room in the basement. Above the bar are a set of cabinets with a big piece of glass. Etched in the corner of the glass is a circle. Inside the circle are the two letters, "TS." I dedicated my bar "To Seth," my friend and mentor. I would not have the life I have today if it weren't for him. He is one of the most generous and giving people that I know. And I am lucky to know him.

CHAPTER 29

I WON

"Winning is a habit." ~Leo Durocher

In January 2007, I achieved a life-long goal.

I was a multi-millionaire in the process of finishing building a 10,000-square-foot house. I had a condo on the beach in Gulf Shores, Alabama. I had a lake house with a boat and two Wave-Runners, and I'd bought my first plane. Yes, I was a financial success, but I was also a personal wreck.

Around this time, I started having some health issues. I couldn't sleep. I had stomach issues all the time. I went to the doctor to figure out what was wrong. He asked me if I was under a lot of stress at work. I laughed and said NO. I had just sold my company, was a multi-millionaire, and basically didn't work anymore. I was living the American Dream. He prescribed sleeping pills and a mild antidepressant. As I left his office, I thought, *why in the world would I need those now!? I needed those for the last twenty years, not now. Everything was supposed to be perfect now.* The truth was after twenty years of high stress, and my marriage falling apart, my body had had enough and started working against me.

Life lesson...

Stress is a killer. I mean it. Stress can actually kill you. It destroys your body slowly over time, and you don't even know it's happening. If you are stressed, you need to figure out how to make it go away. This is critical. You need to figure it out now and not later. Once it tears you apart, it's too late to fix it.

I still owned the insurance call center. We were rolling along and growing each year. I was at a point where I would show up around 10 or 11 AM, go to lunch, and leave around four each day. At this point, I was trying to figure out how to sell the insurance company. I was tired of business. I was tired of the everyday battles. I didn't need the money, and I just wanted to quit.

It took another eighteen months, but we ended up selling the agency to a venture capital group out of California. The deal closed in 2008. I made another million dollars on my split.

Shortly after the sale, I got a call from one of the insurance carriers that we represented. They'd heard I had sold both companies and told me they were struggling to get their internal Direct to Consumer sales call center working properly. They were also struggling with some senior management issues and wanted to know if I would fly up to their headquarters and take a look at their operations. This was a multi-billion-dollar company, and they wanted my advice.

I asked the lady how much they thought my consultation would be worth. She said she would pay me $100,000 for a week's worth of work and a report.

After I hung up the phone, I walked over to Seth's office and told him what had happened. I was going to get $100,000 for one week of work. I was stunned. Seth told me I was an industry expert since I had sold two companies. People would now think I was really smart. That was an amazing feeling.

"The kid who barely got out of high school and dropped out of college, the guy who failed so many times, was now an expert."

I flew up to Milwaukee for a week and wrote my report. When I turned it in, I told the company they had seven critical areas that were broken. Before I even finished my presentation, the CEO stopped me and asked me if I could fix the problems. I told him, "Yes," and he told the lady I was working with to figure out a compensation package for me to consult for them.

Over the next eighteen months, I took a $50 million division that was losing about $1 million a month and turned it profitable. The company ended up paying me around $750,000 for my time, and I was only working about ten days a month.

Over the next two years, I ran consulting projects with several other companies and was paid large sums of money to help them fix their problems. I specifically remember one day being at home and going out to get the mail. There was another check for $100,000. My wife was standing in the kitchen when I opened the envelope and said, "Hey look, another $100,000." I flipped the check over onto the counter and said, "Can you believe it's this easy to make money?" It was crazy. For so many years,

Anita and I struggled to make ends meet, pay bills, and buy food. But there we were sitting at the house with checks just showing up for more money than we used to make in a year.

It dawned on me then that I had won. I had done exactly what I set out to do. I was more financially successful than anyone in my family. I was more successful than anyone I had graduated high school with. I was more successful than any of my friends. I had cars and houses and a plane and lots of toys. I traveled the world.

I should have been happy since I had won the fight, and the battle was over. Nobody could tell me that I wasn't worthy because I had come out on top.

Life lesson...

This is a repeating lesson. It doesn't matter where you started or even where you were a year ago. You have the power to change your life and end up in a completely different place if you want to. If you want it badly enough...nothing else matters. Your story is not even close to being over if you feel discouraged because your journey starts anew every single day.

A funny thing happened around that time. That driving force, that burning desire, the thing that pushed me every minute of every day...faded away. There was nothing left to prove.

I won. I was not a billionaire. I was not even superrich.

But every picture I had put on the refrigerator and every financial dream I'd had over the last 20 years was accomplished. I didn't need to continue fighting.

I remember thinking that I was tired. I was tired of the fighting. I was tired of the stress. I was tired of having to prove myself every day. I was tired of the game. I was tired of business. I just wanted to quit...and I could.

CHAPTER 30

MONEY ISN'T EVERYTHING

"Money is numbers, and numbers never end. If it takes money to be happy, your search for happiness will never end." ~Robert Nesta Marley

I had spent the last twenty years in a battle, every minute, of every hour, of every day, of every year. I was in a battle for success and a battle for my soul.

I was not happy during that time.

I did not know how to have fun.

I was antisocial.

I would attend parties with my wife, go to leave after an hour, and then tell Anita to get a ride home.

I had nothing in common with those people at the parties. I did not have time for parties anyway as I had to think about work and what I was going to do the next day.

I had missed out on life. I was not the best father I could be, and I was a terrible husband. I thought I was doing the right thing by being "all business" all the time. I thought chasing that dream at all costs was how I would eventually be happy. And I wanted to be happy, but it would have to wait until I was successful...at least that's what I thought.

It was 2008, and I had sacrificed my entire life chasing money. Well, I got the money but lost my wife. She wasn't actually gone yet, but the wheels were in motion.

I wanted to learn how to have fun since I'd never learned how, since I hadn't made time for it.

I wanted to learn how to be a real human being. But I was a very disconnected person with very few friends, who was solely focused on business. I wanted to learn how to have friends. In fact, I needed to learn how to do these things.

But now, I wanted to travel and enjoy the success that I had fought for over the past twenty years, to experience the world. And I wanted to do it with my wife.

But she didn't want to do it with me anymore. I had not treated her right for a long time. I was not a good husband. I was not a protector. I did not look out for her and had not been the man I needed to be for two decades. Like a lot of men, I assumed that because I was providing for the family financially, I was doing my job. Unfortunately, I learned too late, that's not really what it's about. Our marriage spun out of control, and we were both miserable.

Still, I could not understand why she had gone through all the negative with me for twenty years but then did not want to enjoy the positive aspects with me.

She could not understand why I would expect her to want to do anything with me after so many years of being a disconnected husband. It got worse every month for a couple of years. Then sometime around March 2011, we both wanted out. The thing that I said I would never do as a kid—that I would never get divorced—was happening to me. We divorced in September of 2012.

Looking back on the situation, and after two years of therapy, I cannot blame her. I take about seventy-five percent of the blame for the demise of my marriage.

In my defense, I did the best I could. Coming from my background with absolutely no example of love, marriage, or relationships, I didn't have a clue as to what I was supposed to do as a husband or father. I am not using my childhood as an excuse because everything in my life is my responsibility. But there is a saying I remember from my days in the Amway business, and I love Amwayisms... This one fits: "Pigs don't know pigs stink." I didn't know what I didn't know.

Here is what I did know. I knew that the way I grew up was not right. I knew that my childhood family relationships were a disaster and destructive. I knew I had to break that cycle of physical abuse I'd endured as a child. These are the things I absolutely knew.

What I didn't know was how to be the person I was supposed to be. And since I couldn't figure it out, I did the only thing I could, which was to leave home and disassociate with my family and not look back.

Then I tried to figure out life on my own.

I did, however, succeed in breaking the cycle of abuse, and I am very proud of that. I have raised amazing children if I do say so myself.

Unfortunately, I could not break other parts of that cycle because I did not know how.

> **"I did not know how to be a truly great man, husband, and father. It takes both experience and guidance to succeed in this way, and I had neither."**

So I did the best I could, but unfortunately, it was not enough for my marriage. After a couple of years of counseling, I figured out what I did wrong, why I did it wrong, how I should've done better, and how I could do better in the future. But it was too late.

Life lesson #1...

Understand what is most important in your life. Your family means more than anything—it especially outranks money. Money is awesome and can provide a wonderful life if used properly, but it is not everything.

I heard a saying that fits here: "I've been poor, and I've been rich, and I will take rich every time"...But it's not worth trading your family for. You can have both, but you have to be happy along the way, or it will not be worth it in the end.

Life lesson #2...

If you have access to someone to help guide you in life and if you have someone who loves you and is there for you to get advice from, use them. Life is so much easier when you have people helping you not to make mistakes.

Last Christmas, I gave my kids each $5,000 in a stock trading account. I told them it was time to learn to invest. My son called me the other day because he had made a mistake trading a couple of stocks and lost some money. He said to me, "Why do my mistakes have to cost me money?" I told him, "Mistakes are how you learn, and learning from them is the key to being successful in the future. If you never fail, you will never succeed. That is just the way it is." Then I helped him correct the mistake, and I am betting he won't make it again.

CHAPTER 31

I WAS WRONG

"The cost of being wrong is less than the cost of doing nothing." ~Seth Godin

As I look back on my divorce and the years to follow, it was a very hard experience for me.

After I moved out of the house, I went up to our lake place to live. I was so depressed that I only got out of bed to eat and drink and then went back to bed. I was a total wreck.

And it was weird because I was so super successful financially at this point and yet was a total failure personally. I didn't have anyone to talk to or confide in. My twenty years of all work and no play had left me with no friends—only employees and acquaintances.

This period of depression lasted about a month. After that, I started counseling and trying to figure out how I could either fix what I was feeling or at least not be so miserable. I was in counseling for two years.

Now I have said that every bad experience in my life has ultimately led to something good. So the question here is, *what good was going to come out of my divorce?*

Here's what I have learned so far.

The divorce forced me to low points in my life personally, mentally, and emotionally. A powerful thing happens when a person gets to a low point in their life. When you hit rock bottom and have no place to go, the walls that you have built over time come down. The walls that you used to store your very core beliefs and to either protect yourself or to lean on to fight off the world go away.

You realize that maybe those walls of protection were actually keeping things out that needed to be in there with you instead of them protecting you from harm. Your core beliefs get challenged. Hitting rock bottom is the first step to making actual functional change. Superficial change is easy, but in times of stress, we all duck behind the walls we have built and hide out, refusing to listen and learn. Those walls have to come down for us to change, and hitting rock bottom is the only way to get to the point of being able to receive that change. Once you are there, you can get rid of the old ways of thinking and start putting new and better stuff in your brain. Then you can rebuild the healthy foundational walls that you should lean on moving forward.

Life lesson...

If you're about to hit rock bottom, make sure you put yourself in the presence of someone who is willing, qualified, and can help you. You are in a state of weakness, and you do not want the wrong infor-

178

mation, or advice, getting into your mind while you start building new healthy walls. Because once the new information or new beliefs are in there, behind those new walls, they are not leaving unless you hit rock bottom again. The changes that you need to make, will depend on the people and information you put in your mind. Be very selective of what you allow to be in your mind behind those walls.

When I hit my personal rock bottom as an adult, my core beliefs were challenged. Everything I thought I knew about being a man, an adult, a husband, and a father was clearly wrong. I needed to change. So, I went to counseling. However, I didn't just go; I threw myself into it. I wanted to know what books my counselor read and what books she studied in school and in continuing education. When I found out, I bought those books and read them between sessions. I wanted to understand why my counselor said the things she said, so I could figure this counseling thing out.

Along the way, I did start to see my weaknesses and where my thinking was off. I started to understand what my wife wanted in a husband and how I should have treated her. I learned how to calm down and that I didn't always have to be right. I learned...for two years.

I am not saying by any means that I figured it all out, but I did change from the person I was back then. I am more patient. I am more tolerant of different thinking. I became a better boss to my employees. I have heard many times now: "Wow, you have changed."

> ## "Although I have said often that I would never go to counseling, I am glad I did."

I have made tremendous progress in these areas over the past couple of years. If there is a positive in my divorce, it is that I have become a better man, a better father, and a better partner to whomever I will end up with. I wish that I had been able to do this before I got divorced. I wish that I had not broken my family. I wish that I could live in Disney World. But wishes are for fairy godmothers. They are not real. This is the life I have, and I intend to make the second half of it better than the first. This is my journey.

Life lesson...

People can change. I know you hear all the time that people can't, but they can. It might take a devastating event in their life, or they might have to hit rock bottom, but believe me, they can change.

CHAPTER 32

WHO IS MY FATHER?

*"I have four children. Two are adopted.
I forget which two." ~Bob Constantine*

Growing up sucked.

I had an abusive stepfather and a man who I thought was my father who was not engaged or connected. The man who I thought was my father was about 5′ 8″ tall. He had jet black hair on the sides and was mostly bald on top. I was 5′ 11″ with blondish red hair. My supposed father had three sons with his new wife. All of them were short, with dark, balding hair. In the family pictures, you can see four short, balding guys and one taller guy with reddish-blond hair. Something just didn't feel right.

I did not look a thing like anybody. I'd had a nagging feeling my whole life that I didn't belong in this family. When I was in my teens, I would hint around with him and my mother about their marriage, when exactly they'd gotten divorced and when my mother met my stepdad, but I could never get a straight answer. I would even ask about the blood types in the family, trying to figure it out on my own—still, no answers. My parents just weren't being straight with me.

When my kids were small, I used to joke about it with them. I would say things like, "Hey, you need to call your grandfather...if he is your grandfather." This was a constant theme whenever I talked about him.

One day, after my family and I had returned from skiing in Breckenridge and we were in the airport coming home, my daughter was leaning up against a wall playing with her phone —not paying attention to me. I made a comment about calling her grandfather when we got back, and I ended it the way I always did: "...if he is your grandfather." She didn't even look up at me when she replied, "Why don't you just ask him?" She just went back to her game, and that was the end of that conversation. It was February of 2011.

One month later, in March, my marriage fell apart.

I had moved out of the house, and my life was a wreck. I was about to head into town one day to meet one of the managers who worked for me for lunch when I got a Fed Ex package. It was my divorce papers. That was a bad day. I went ahead to the lunch anyway. I also happened to be in the middle of a lawsuit with my best friend from college who I loaned $250,000 to buy a business up in Ohio. He stole the money, and I had to sue him. My trial date was the following week in northern Ohio.

In one week, I had been served divorce papers and was prepping for a court date.

When I was at lunch, I thought, *hey, as long as my world is falling apart, why not see if I can toss another grenade on my life story and blow this thing up.*

So I picked up my phone and texted my mother. I said, "I am going up to Ohio next week, and I'm going to do a DNA test with my half-brother. I want to know if Jim is my father." Her response was: "Can I call you?" I responded, "No...just answer the question." Her response: "No."

I remember saying out loud in this restaurant..."HOLY SHIT!!" I was loud enough that people looked over at us. I texted her back. "Is my stepfather my real father?" She said, "No." So, I asked, "Who is my father?" She said, "His name is Daniel," and texted me a picture of him. She actually had a picture handy that she could text me! She had been waiting for this conversation her whole life and was ready. *Wow...* Add that to the list of things I was dealing with that week.

I did a little internet research and found a potential person who could be my father up in northern Ohio, strangely enough about three miles from the courthouse where the trial was scheduled. I had my lawyer up in Ohio try to contact this person with the message: "I'm trying to locate a Daniel who worked at AT&T in the 60s."

My lawyer had no luck getting ahold of this person. But I had the address where he lived, so when I went up for my court case, I drove over to the house in a trailer park. When I found the address, I pulled into the driveway. His car was there. Let me explain how I knew it was his car.

Growing up, I had vanity plates on my car. They had my initials with the number "9" afterward. My plates were BSW 9. When I pulled into the driveway, the car sitting there had the license plates DST 9. It was weird. Imagine how I felt walking up to the door of a potential father I had never met at the age of forty-five.

I knocked on the door, and nobody answered. But I had a phone number, so I called it. No answer again. Then I left. I had some time to kill before the court case, so I went to McDonald's to wait. While I was sitting there, my phone rang. It was him. I answered, and he said, "Yeah, you just called me. What do you want?" I told him I was trying to locate Daniel, who worked at AT&T in the sixties. He said, "What do you want?"

**"I told him I was trying to locate my father.
His response was quick. 'I'm not your father...'
and he hung up. Well, that settled it for me.
I knew it was him. His was not a normal response.
It was a guilty response."**

Next, I went to Facebook, and in about five minutes, I found him and his family. He had an ex-wife, a daughter, and a son.

I Facebook messaged all three of them with the same message stating that I was looking for Daniel, who had worked at AT&T in the sixties. I got a response back from Lisa, his daughter. She said, "That is my dad. How can I help you?" I told her I thought we were related and was trying to confirm that he was the right person. She said it was and then asked me what side of the family I was on. In other words, "Who were my parents?" I responded that she might want to sit down for this one and then typed back that I thought she was my sister. I often wonder what she thought at the very second she read that. It must have been a surreal moment.

It took her eight hours to reply. She then sent me a message asking me why I thought that. I told her that my mother had told me that she'd had an affair with her father, gotten pregnant, and I was born. She also said that he knew about me. I told her that I hadn't found out about him until that week. Her next response was not expected. She told me she had been talking to her mother and father all day. Her father absolutely denied that I was his son, but she didn't believe him. She told me when she looked at my Facebook pictures; her jaw hit the floor. I was a dead ringer for Daniel. She didn't need any more proof. I also talked to her mother, who told me she couldn't believe it either. She said I looked exactly like Daniel.

That conversation began a wonderful relationship with my sister Lisa and her husband, Matt. Over the years, I got to know them, as well as some of my cousins in Ohio. Bio-dad, however, still refused to admit I was his son. He would get angry with Lisa when she brought me up. I also have a brother, Gary, who I have never met. He still has no interest in meeting me.

Then two years ago, I was down at my place in Clearwater Beach, Florida, when I got a call from bio-dad. I picked up the phone and said, "Hello." He said, "Brian?" I answered, "Yes?" And he said, "I want to meet you."

I was a bit shocked, after five years and many fights with my sister about me not being his son, he wanted to meet me. I told him I was down in Florida but that I would come up to Ohio in a couple of months, and we could meet. He told me he wanted to meet me right then and that he would drive from Ohio down to Florida that weekend and meet me Monday. I agreed and told him where I was. Now, all I had to do was wait for him to call me that coming Monday.

I hung up the phone, called Lisa, and said: "Guess who just called me?" When I told her, she was shocked. She told me she hadn't talked to him since Easter six weeks earlier when she'd gotten into an argument about me, and he'd stormed out of Easter dinner and went home. "I'll be amazed if he actually shows up," she told me.

Monday came around, and I got a call from Daniel, saying he was in Clearwater, and we should grab lunch. We agreed on a time and place, and I headed over there.

In the previous five years, while he had denied I existed, I had told Lisa that I wanted to just show up at the next family reunion. My idea was to walk in and sit down next to him. I would introduce myself and ask him if he still wanted to deny that he was my father.

I know I was a little bit angry when I thought of this plan. But over the last five years, I had played out the scene in my head many times even though I had no idea how I would react when I finally met him. It would be interesting.

I was already at the restaurant sitting outside when Daniel came in. I recognized him, but he didn't recognize me. He came over, and we introduced ourselves and sat down. I have to tell you there was no anger in me. It was strangely calm in my soul. This was an open wound, an open question that was getting healed. A chapter that had haunted me my whole life and particularly, in the last five years, was about to close. We talked for two hours about his past and mine. I asked him, "Why are you coming forward now? Why, after five years, did you call me out of the blue?"

Now, Lisa had told me that at Easter dinner, when my name came up, Daniel got mad and said I was not his son. Lisa and her mother, however, were having none of that. Lisa told him that he had told her all her life to own up to her mistakes, and he wasn't doing that. Her mother told him he had children and grandchildren that he was ignoring, and that wasn't right. He needed to step up and own it. When Daniel heard that, he got mad and left.

When I asked Daniel why now, he told me that his brother was dying. His sister and brother both had cancer, and he might have it as well. He told me that he needed to get a few things right in his life...and I was the first thing that he needed to get right.

After that lunch, I invited him out to the beach to have dinner with me. He accepted, and we talked over dinner that night and met again for lunch the next day. The entire experience was interesting. If I had to give it a word, it would be "familiar." Meaning there was a familiar feeling about being with him. Daniel left and went back to Ohio, and I didn't hear from him for another five days.

Then my phone rang, and there he was again... I answered, and Daniel asked me if I would be willing to take a DNA test. He said he had already set it up at a local place, and all I had to do was show up. It would take five minutes. I agreed and went the next day. At the DNA place, they did a mouth swab and sent me home. Now all I had to do was wait. Two days later, I got an email. It said, "Daniel IS the biological father of Brian Will."

There you go... Forty-five years to figure it out... Five years for him to admit it... Five minutes for a DNA test to close that chapter for good. Daniel is my biological father.

The next week my phone rang again.

Daniel asked if I would be willing to fly up to Ohio and go to the family reunion, the very family reunion that I had dreamed about showing up to so I could confront him.

Now, he was inviting me.

I agreed and called my sister Lisa to ask if she was going. She said she wasn't and asked me why I wanted to know. I told her what happened, and she was again in shock. Her words were: "For five years he got mad at anyone in the family who would bring you up, and now he invites you to meet them? This I have to see."

The following Saturday, I flew up to Ohio in my plane. Lisa picked me up, and we went to the reunion.

As soon as I got there, I sat down with Lisa and Matt, then Daniel came over to get me and said, "I have to introduce you around." He took me by the arm and led me over to his dying brother and said, "I want to introduce you to Brian. He is my son."

The entire day was spent meeting relatives who already knew about me but were meeting me for the first time. It was yet another experience in my life that I don't believe a lot of people ever have, and it added another chapter to my life.

After a fake father who didn't really care about me, an abusive stepfather who threw me out, and a bio-dad who denied me for fifty years (adamantly for the last five), this man stood there proud to introduce me as his son. It was weird. This scene played out over and over for the next thirty minutes. Everyone knew who I was and kept telling me they were glad to finally meet me. It was an interesting day.

Daniel and I traded texts occasionally after that, but I didn't really see him at all for the next two years. Lisa and I talk now and then and trade Facebook messages. Things went back to normal. I thought that was the end of that story...and then I went to Japan.

A couple of years earlier, I had taken a 23andMe test. My kids and ex-wife did it as well. I never thought much about it. Then in the spring of 2019, I took my son to Japan for his semester abroad for college. One day while we were there, I was in bed about to go to sleep when I got a Facebook message. The message said, "Hi, my name is Tim, and the strangest thing just happened. I did a 23andMe test, and it came back that you are my half-brother... That can't be possible, can it?"

Now the story goes, Tim was at dinner with his wife earlier that day when his daughter from another marriage called and told him she was thinking of doing a 23andMe test. She jokingly wanted to know if any other siblings would show up. Tim laughed and told her he didn't think so and hung up. His wife then commented that he had done the test, and had he ever looked at the results, to which he replied that he hadn't checked it out in several years. She said, "Well, why don't you look and see what's on there? Maybe you have a long-lost relative that will show up." So, Tim logged into the app. He was so shocked at what he found that he dropped his phone on the table and went white as a ghost. His wife asked him what the heck was wrong, and he showed her. "I have a brother."

There I was in Tokyo having almost the same experience Lisa had had seven years earlier with me. I asked Tim to call me and talk. When he called, the first thing I asked him was, "Are you sure you want to go down this rabbit hole? Because you are about to find things out about your mother that you may not want to know." Now Tim had been in law enforcement all his life after the Marines. He told me he could handle it, and we talked some more. Without getting into too much detail, Tim learned a lot about his family. He has another sister and brother as well.

Lisa was the only one who had not done the DNA test, so she, along with Tim's other brother, went ahead and did it. The results came back that Lisa was also a half-sister, and his other brother that Tim thought was a full brother was only a half-brother. Talk about an eye-opener.

Tim contacted Daniel to see if he would meet. Daniel was again shocked but agreed. I flew up to Ohio, and Tim, Lisa, Daniel and I all met for lunch. I called it "Daniel's Offspring Lunch." It was a good day. It was nice to meet Tim. He is a good guy. We jokingly asked Daniel if any more kids would show up, and his answer was, "I don't know. They might." So, if you're reading this...who knows...you might be my sibling... Daniel was a looker and a player!!!

Life lesson...

Be nice to strangers. They might be your brother or sister!!!

Fake Dad

To back up a bit in my story, after my original encounter on the phone with Daniel, I went to my court date for the lawsuit against my college best friend.

I won the case, although he went bankrupt afterward, and I never collected.

Anyway...after the case, I headed down to Columbus—which was only about an hour by car—to go find Joe (the one I thought was my father my whole life). I found him at a bar around 2 PM. He was half-drunk and sitting outside, smoking a cigarette. This was a pretty typical place to find him on most days.

As I got out of my car and walked up to him, he did a double-take and asked what I was doing there. I told him I needed to talk to him. His response was, "Hold on. Let me finish my cigarette." After his smoke, we went inside and sat down. He asked me what was up. I told him that I had just found out some interesting news. It appeared he wasn't my father. I will never forget his response. Joe reached over and put his hand on my arm. He kind of laughed and said, "Well, what took you so long to figure that out??!!" I questioned, "So you knew?" He told me yes.

Back in 1964, Joe (fake dad) worked at AT&T along with my mother, Daniel (bio-dad), and stepfather (the evil one). One day a lady came to the office and asked if she could speak to Joe. When he said yes, she handed him a letter. The letter told him that I wasn't his son and that Daniel was. Joe told me he had no idea who that lady was and didn't have a copy of the letter, but that is when he found out. I asked him why he'd never told me even though I had hinted around about the subject my whole life. He told me it wasn't his responsibility to tell me—that it was my mother's. I was stunned and haven't spoken to him since then. He was never a real father when I was growing up, and he perpetuated a lie for forty-five years. Then when confronted with it...he laughed.

I also haven't spoken to my ex-half-brothers. They are very angry with me as if this is my fault. One of them even called and threatened me. He also phoned my mother in a drunken state and called her some very vile names. The entire situation is very sad.

Life lesson...

Lying to your children is never a good idea. Lying to them about something so big...only to have them find out decades later is even worse. Just tell them the truth. They will respect you more and get over it more easily than if they had been subjected to a lifetime of lies and deceit.

CHAPTER 33

I CAN'T BELIEVE
HE TOOK THE DEAL

"You're afraid, like I make my deals with the devil."
~From the song, "A Day to Remember"

One night in 2009, I was sitting in a bar with a couple of people who had worked for me in one of the companies that I had sold. Nancy, who was my accountant and also at the bar that night, looked at me and said, "Why don't you buy a bar? You love bars." My immediate response was, "Go find me a bar and I will buy it."

The next day Nancy called and told me that the bar we had been sitting in was for sale. The following week, I owned it! Now, I knew absolutely nothing about running a bar or a restaurant. I bought it because I pictured myself like Sam Malone on *Cheers*. I would hang out at the end of the bar, and "everybody would know my name" (insert theme song here).

I was in the restaurant business with no clue what I was doing. I'd just jumped in as I always had and tried to figure out how to make money. The first year I lost around $50,000. To put it bluntly, I was not "winning."

Around this time, I got a call from the broker who had sold me the bar. He told me he had four more bars called The Derby for sale. They were asking $800,000 for all four. I asked him to send me the financials to look at it.

After assessing everything and talking to the various landlords, it became apparent that the owner, Bob, was in big trouble. The landlords were going to evict him on all his properties the following Monday...which was only four days away. He was six months and $160,000 behind on rent. He had two tax liens totaling $180,000 that he owed to the IRS and another $105,000 that he owed to the state. He owed $20,000 to the bank for an overdue loan, another $60,000 to a merchant financing company, and hadn't paid his food bills of $50,000 or his payroll of around $50,000 for the last two weeks. Everyone was about to sue him and drive him into bankruptcy.

Life Lesson...

Never buy something without doing your due diligence. Just because somebody is giving you a price doesn't mean they won't take less... sometimes a LOT less.

Bob was not the guy who had started these bars. Bobs' dad, Bob Senior, had. Bob was forty years old, and he'd never had a job other than working for his dad behind the bar. When Bob Senior died eighteen months earlier, Bob took over the bar. Unfortunately, **"Bob had no idea how to run a business, and** eighteen months after his father passed, Bob had burned through probably $1.2 million in proceeds and hadn't paid his bills. Bob was in big trouble and needed a way out."

All I saw was blood in the streets and an opportunity for creative solutions. I made Bob an offer on the Thursday before Halloween in 2010.

This was my offer:

- I would give him $0. (Not the $800,000 he asked for).

- He would sign over all the businesses to me by noon of that day and walk away. He would not take any cash out of the registers or food or alcohol from the locations.

- I would let him drink at any of the bars for half price for six months.

- In return, I would negotiate down his debt for him with all the related parties I stated above.

He agreed to the deal. Then showed up with a drink in his hand to sign the paperwork. I couldn't believe it. I'd just acquired four restaurants doing nearly $4 million in revenue for $0. *Wow…*

Life lesson...

I could have assumed that Bob wouldn't take zero dollars and offered $50,000-100,000, which still would have been a good deal for me, but remember my other life lesson: if your first offer doesn't insult them, you offered too much. So I offered $0, and he took it. In doing so, I saved myself $50,000-100,000. Business is brutal, so ALWAYS low-ball because you have nothing to lose.

Over the course of the next three months, I kept my word and got the IRS and the state of Georgia to drop the liens... The banks dropped their claims, and the food vendors wrote off their bills. We got him out of over $600,000 in debt.

I was now in the restaurant business and scoring four out of five. Meaning four of the locations were making money, and one was losing it.

CHAPTER 34

I THOUGHT I WAS SMART

"I'm not saying you're stupid. I'm just saying you've got bad luck when it comes to thinking." ~Unknown

Soon after this deal, I ended up selling the first restaurant that was losing money. I then found another location that I wanted to acquire. After purchasing that location, we changed the name to the brand we owned.

With that deal done, we made the decision to build another new location from scratch. We also bought another location that was about two hours away from our home base in Atlanta. It was in trouble, and we thought we could turn it around.

We now had seven locations, and my empire was growing. Unfortunately, I still had a lot to learn about the restaurant business and was about to take a hit.

The new location we built was in a Publix shopping complex and across the street from a very popular regional chain in Atlanta. It was about three miles from a downtown historic district that also had a bunch more restaurants and shops. The regional brand

197

across the street was doing around $3 million in revenue. But our food was better, and I really thought I had a winner.

The location I bought and that I changed to our name had been in that location for ten years. I figured a simple name change couldn't hurt us, especially since we had better food.

The final location that we bought two hours away from us was in Macon, Georgia. I thought this was a good decision because I figured...*how hard can it be to manage an existing team?*

Six months later, the location where I changed the name crashed. It was a disaster from day one. I took away everything that had been built over the last ten years and changed it. Then the people stopped coming in. I ended up closing that location six months later, although I had to pay rent on the building for another year. That cost me $180,000.

The location in Macon was failing for other reasons; the staff didn't care, and the place was a mess. We tried to get down there to make changes, but I didn't have my trusted team in place there as I had at other locations, and we didn't have enough time to do all the traveling required to get it into good financial shape. Six months later, I closed that location, too, taking a loss of about $70,000.

The location that I built cost $250,000, and I lost $100,000 a year for the next two years. I was $450,000 into that location and wound up selling it for $80,000. My total loss on those three locations was $620,000 over those two years.

Here is what I learned about the restaurant business. You have to be a brand that people know well, or you have to be in a destination that people naturally go to, or you have to be extremely lucky to succeed. I wasn't any of those. You also need to under-stand why a location is failing and know when NOT to try to stop it. The regional location across the street with their inferior food watched me come and go without missing a beat. They were a brand that people recognized. The restaurants in the historic district also didn't miss a beat because they had thousands of people walking around them daily due to their location. The location that was two hours away was just a bad deal.

"It was 2011, and four out of the seven locations were doing okay. My last three locations were failing quickly. I was at fifty-seven percent success."

Life lesson...

Success in one area does not make you a genius in other areas.

A few more years went by, and I got a call from my broker friend. He had another deal he wanted me to look at. This restaurant had been around for ten years. I agreed to look at it but determined I WOULD NOT change the name. The owner wanted $300,000. After looking over the deal, I offered $200,000. The owner wouldn't take it, and I walked away. A year later, the broker came back to me and said the owner would take my $200,000. I laughed and told him I would give him $100,000. The owner again refused, and I walked away. Another year passed, and the broker came back again. Now, the owner said he would take my $100,000.

This location was doing around $1 million in sales, and by this time, I could figure out the reason the spot was working—it was a brand. It had been there for ten years and was well known.

The $100,000 was a good deal for me. The problem for him was that I was seeing blood in the streets again, which meant more opportunity. My offer this time was zero dollars. I would take over, purchase his inventory, and give him his lease deposit back. That was my deal. Now, remember my life lesson about low-balling offers and insulting people on the first go around. That's what I was doing.

The owner called back and said he couldn't take my offer. The problem for him was that I knew that he had taken a job offer that was forcing him to move. He had to go. He also had to either re-sign his new lease, or he was out of the space. I knew he was not about to re-sign since he was being transferred. With all this information, I had him. We continued to negotiate, and in the end, I paid him $10,000. This was a killer deal. We didn't change the name of that location as it had averaged over $100,000 a year in gross profits for the last four years. I knew better now.

Life lesson...

Do your homework. Understand ALL the variables before you sign a deal. Do not feel bad about making the best deal for you. Nobody else is looking out for you. You have to look out for yourself and your family.

This story reminds me of something my son said to me not too long ago. He was talking about people buying things without looking at all their options. He called that kind of person an "uninformed buyer." Now my son is the guy who, when he sets out to buy something, spends an hour comparing it to everything in the world. That's not me, and I am not a fan of shopping with him, but his point is valid. It applies not just to small things but to large deals as well. The point? Be an informed buyer.

CHAPTER 35

SOMETIMES YOU WIN. SOMETIMES YOU...LEARN

"Sometimes you win. Sometimes you ~~lose~~ learn."
~Robert T. Kiyosaki

My team and I were hitting five out of eight in the restaurant business. That was until we found out that one of our locations was in a building that was being rezoned for apartments. It was going to be sold and torn down. This left us with four operating locations, so we decided it was time to expand again.

This time we used the knowledge we had gained over the years to select two more locations to build new restaurants that were in what is called mixed-use developments. We call them live, work, and play communities. They are destinations, and basically, a development that has office buildings, apartments, and homes as well as retail shops and restaurants all within the confines of the development. You can walk out your front door and go to work, go shopping, or go out to eat.

The new brand we launched in the community developments was called Central City Tavern. We decided to do an upscale tavern aesthetic on these locations with a sports theme. The two new locations were in fairly new communities, and they were booming. When we got both of those up and running, they were a smashing success. They were generating an additional $4.5 million in revenue, which more than doubled our revenue on the previous locations. We had a winner.

We are currently building three more locations in the same type of mixed-use developments around the metro area. Revenues will top $15 million, and we will employ around 300 people when they are all complete.

**"Most people have heard the phrase:
'Sometimes you win, and sometimes you lose.'
I hate that saying. You should never lose."**

Success has a fundamental foundation in failure. It is required to learn and grow. Every failure should be the building block of knowledge that you use to get to the next level.

This situation reminds me of a story about my daughter when she was little. She had hurt herself and was in pain. I remember she was crying and asked me, "Daddy, why do we have to have pain?!!"

I explained that pain is your protection mechanism to keep you from really hurting yourself too badly. For instance, "What if you didn't feel pain and you put your hand on a hot stove? What would happen to your hand?" I asked her. She replied, "It would burn up." I told her, "Yes, and then you wouldn't have a hand, would you?" She agreed. "Now, you know why pain is important," I told her. "You want to keep your hand, and the pain is telling you to stop doing what you're doing before you lose your hand!! ...So, thank God for pain!!" She liked that answer and went away happy.

I am amazed at how many people don't learn from pain. They make the same mistakes over and over without learning. They are the definition of "Sometimes you win, and sometimes you lose." The problem is they never grow from their experience and never get better. You should always take a step back from every failure and learn. Ask yourself, *why did it fail? What went wrong? How can I not fail like that again?*

Life, business, relationships, and pretty much everything you go through in your life should be a learning experience. Always try to do better than the last time. Embrace your failures and pain so you can be a better person or a better business person in the future. Pain and failure are good.

Life lesson...

Sometimes you win, and sometimes you learn.

CHAPTER 36

TODAY

"Life isn't about finding yourself. Life is about creating yourself." ~George Bernard Shaw

As I sit here writing this, I am out in Park City, Utah, for a month on a ski vacation. My business at home is humming along, and my team is working diligently on my behalf. I have created a business and lifestyle that doesn't require me to actually have to go to work. My daughter always tells me, "Daddy, you're not normal." I can travel, hang out at my beach place, the lake house, or here in Park City, and our business will continue to grow. Technology has allowed me to manage everything from my phone and occasionally my computer. I have hired a great team of people who are passionate about what we do, and I trust them. I also manage them, but I trust them. I am not a billionaire. I don't have Ferraris in the garage at home, although I do have a Tesla...greatest car ever!! I'm not even the richest guy I know... but I have created something that gives me a certain amount of freedom.

My children are doing great. My daughter is married now and works for her alma mater traveling around the country, working with other alumni. My son is about to graduate from the University of Tennessee with an international business degree and a focus on Japanese. He spent five months in Tokyo earlier this year and has plans to go back to Japan and teach English to young students for a year after graduation. My kids rock. I successfully sheltered them from my past and upbringing. They are living great lives.

CHAPTER 37

WHAT WAS THE POINT OF ALL THIS?

"I'm writing a book. I've got the page numbers done."
~Steven Wright

So the question that remains is... *What was the point of this book?*

It was a goal of mine. I absolutely believe in writing down your goals and looking at them every day.

Writing this book has been written on every goal sheet I'd created over the last ten years. Every day for the past five years since I started writing it, finishing it was on my goal sheet. I looked at it every day...and every day, in every year that passed, I said to myself, *this is the year I'm going to finish it.*

I originally sat down to write this book, so I could pass it on to my kids. I wanted them to read my stories and have a better understanding of their father. They have only been around the last twenty-five years or so, and I had thirty years of life before that to tell them about. I wanted to give them something so they could go back and read about my life and remember me after I'm gone. I also wanted to pass on life lessons to them and their children. It is one thing to simply tell them. It is quite another to have these lessons in writing to be able to refer back to.

Let's be honest; I'm about fifty-five years old now, and I am in what I call the back twenty-five percent of my life. My time here is limited. I have talked about writing this book for a long time and never did. After I began writing it, I decided that instead of just using words to relay these lessons to my kids, I would tie everything together using stories to make the point. Isn't that how we learn anyway, through stories and experiences?

This book took five years to start and finish. It was a long-term goal that I never gave up on… It just needed the right circumstances for it to all come together, and I wasn't ready when I first had the idea to write it. It just wasn't the right time.

As I was finishing up writing it, I realized that there is another book in me that will focus on business, sales and management, and negotiating and making deals. These are some of my favorite things to do.

"People have hobbies. My hobby is business. I like starting businesses; I like growing them. I like fixing them. It's fun for me. I don't mind working all the time. It's part of my life."

Life lesson...

Sometimes it takes years to accomplish a goal. Don't be discouraged if your goals don't come fast or easy. Don't drop them just because you didn't get them done when you wanted to. I sat on this half-finished book for five years. Now, it's done. I get to check off writing my book from the list, and that is exciting for me!

210

CHAPTER 38

CONCLUSION

"Courage is the power to let go of the familiar."
~Raymond Lindquist

In conclusion, I want to say that life is what you make it.

It doesn't matter where you started.

It doesn't matter what issues you have or what roadblocks are in your way.

It doesn't matter who told you NO or that you can't do it.

It doesn't matter who your parents are or if they are rich or poor.

What you do with your life is still up to you. On a scale of 1-10, it doesn't matter if you started out in life at a five, ten, or in my case at zero. None of that matters. Wherever you are, and wherever you started, your journey begins there.

You can make your life fun, or you can make it suck. Whatever you want to do, you can, as long as you're willing to sacrifice something to get it. The trick is to decide what you want. Then you need to decide what you're willing to give up to get it. It might be money. It might be sleep. It might be free time to play golf, or hang out with your friends. No matter what it is, everything worthwhile will require you to give up something else to get it. A friend once told me, "**You can do anything, but you can't do everything**." That is part of my problem. I want to do everything. I want to go everywhere and see everything there is to see. So, I am going to do my best to see if I can make that happen.

I guess it gets back to the kid and the old man and the water... If I want it as bad as that kid needed to breathe...maybe...just maybe I can make it happen...

"Everyone has a journey....this one is mine."

CHAPTER 39

LIFE LESSONS' SUMMARY

"A hungry stomach, an empty wallet, and a broken heart teach you the most valuable lessons in life."
~Robin Williams

Supplemental life lesson Number 1... *No matter where you are in life as you're reading this, it doesn't have to be too late for you. Understand what is most important in your life and go make it happen*

***

I wanted to summarize the life lessons in a central place in this book so you can read or look them up easily. I have arranged them according to how they appeared in the chapters.

Life Lesson #1... *Don't judge people's future by what you see today. Lots of great people started at the bottom and worked their way up...and lots of people at the top...worked their way down.*

Life lesson #2... *Physical abuse is bad...but so is mental abuse. The words you say to people are incredibly powerful. Words can stay with you for life. Children especially will take your words as the absolute gospel and create their life around how you think of them. You can make a comment to someone, and it has the power to affect their life forever. So watch what you say. And if you realize you said something wrong, take it back immediately before it's too late.*

Life lesson #3... *You have to let go. If somebody does you wrong, you have to let go. If they hurt you or abuse you, you have to let it go. If you truly want that situation in your life to be gone as hard as it is and as much as you don't want to, you have to let it go and move on. Otherwise, the very thing that you hate will stay with you for the rest of your life. It will control you. It will affect everything you do. It will damage every relationship you are in. It will affect the people that you love. It will affect your children and grandchildren. If you do not let it go, you are allowing your pain and its consequences to move on to the next generation. If that happens, it is your fault and nobody else's. Let it go and move on.*

Life lesson #4... *Believe in your kids—even if their ideas are crazy. Even if you don't really believe in them—do it anyway. Encourage them. Support them. What is the worst that can happen? They'll try and fail, sure, but they will still know that if they want to try something else, you will be there to believe in them again. On the other hand, the best that could happen is they succeed as I did. You don't want to be the parent whose child is mad at you after they succeed because you didn't encourage them along the way. You also don't want to be the* *parent whose child doesn't succeed and who loses all hope because you didn't believe in them either. You don't want to be the parent whose child proves you right by failing. They will hate you for that as well.*

Life lesson #5... *Being a hammer isn't necessary. It may work to resolve whatever issue you are facing, but the devastation you will leave behind in your life and in other's lives is not worth it. I had no friends when I was a hammer. I wasn't succeeding as I wanted, and I wasn't a good husband but was a mess. I was not happy, and it took a lot of years, a lot of failures, a lot of lawsuits, and a lot of sleepless nights to get past that. And it took finally meeting another man I could look up to, who showed me how to be a businessperson without being a complete jerk. That's when my life really started improving...*

Life lesson #6... *I had to come to terms with the fact that it would be okay to let my children fail. I would have to stand back and watch it unfold, far enough away that my children felt like they were on their own and making their own decisions, but I would still be close enough to catch them when or if they fell. My job as a father is to pick my children back up and send them on their way, hopefully, smarter, wiser, and only bruised, not broken. That is tough to do. I hope my children learn that lesson and practice that same patience with their own children.*

Life lesson #7... *Whatever your issue is, it doesn't have to slow you down. You only need to learn to focus on your strengths. Then strive to understand your limitations and find the right tool or bring in the right person or people to handle what you can't or don't want to* do. As I like to say: "I have people, and they do the actual work. I am just flying around at 30,000 feet, managing the big picture."

Life lesson #8... *Having specific goals can change your life. They changed mine in the eighth grade, and I didn't even understand the power of goals back then. Now, I know they are powerful, and that writing them down is even more powerful. I've written down my goals for the last thirty-five years. Today, I put them in my iPhone in the notes sections. They are written down as short-term, medium-term, and long-term goals that I break down by year. It's amazing how many goals I have accomplished. Doing this is like magic. You write your goals down, and then your subconscious helps you make them happen.*

Life lesson #9... *If you want it, you have to work for it. Hard work, persistence, and a burning desire can put you on an even playing field with people who have natural talent. You may have to work harder than someone else to get what you want, but you can still get it if you want it bad enough. You can do almost anything you want if you are willing to put in the effort, focus and take the time necessary to do it...even if you have to start from the bottom... And if you need motivation and can't find it, maybe you need to get mad!*

Life lesson #10... *It's important to show, teach, and help your children experience success, so they understand what it feels like to be good at something—so they learn what it's like to succeed. They need that feeling. It drives them to bigger aspirations in their future.*

216

Life lesson #11... *You have no idea what impact or influence you may have on someone. They will probably never tell you either. It may be positive or negative. Your influence may save their life or steer them in a direction that will change their life. Always be aware of the influence you may have on other people. You may not even know that people look up to you and watch your actions. But they do.*

Life lesson #12... *You need to be very protective of your children, know who you are leaving them with, and talk to them about what happens in their life. You need to understand that there are very bad people in the world, and your job as a parent is to keep them safe to the best of your ability.*

In forty years, you do not want to read about horrible things that happened to your children that they never told you because they were afraid!

Life lesson #13... *Sometimes you have to adjust your goals midstream. Sometimes you have to come to the realization that maybe the path you are on is not the best path for you. Just because you started in one direction doesn't mean you have to finish it. If you find out that the end is not going to be what you want, it is okay to change your goal. I'm not saying that you should make this decision lightly, but sometimes you do need to quit, change direction, and find a new path. I see far too many budding young or old entrepreneurs who are stuck with their vision. They can't see past the fact that their dream isn't working, and they continue down the same path of failure until it's too late. Then they blame fate, bad luck, or the fact that they "just can't catch a break."*

Sometimes you need to improvise and adapt, change direction, and find another way. Don't let your vision blind your common sense.

Life lesson #14... *You don't need an education or a head start of any kind to be successful. You just have to work and figure it out along the way.*

Life lesson #15... *You have to constantly improvise and adapt, or today's success will be tomorrow's failure. Every good idea will be copied by someone else, and they will probably do it cheaper than you, or put you under just for spite.*

Life lesson #16... *Raise your kids. Kids want to be raised. They want help and your advice even when they fight it. Kids need you. Yes, you will screw up and sometimes be a bad example. You will even give them the wrong advice at times. But that is far better than abandoning their mental and emotional development when they need it the most. Do your best... Raise your kids... They are begging for it.*

Life lesson #17... *Who you know can be just as important as any-thing else you have going for you. Never underestimate the power of friends. They can make or break you. Networking is a powerful tool in your success. So go make friends and not enemies.*

Life lesson #18... *Music is important!! Okay, that's not really a life lesson... But still, music is important!!*

Life lesson #19... *This situation reminds me of the takeaway close. If someone wants something...tell them they can't have it...take it away... It generally makes them want it even more. I use it all the time in sales. It is an easy way to get someone to demand to take what you are offering. Although, it generally only works on weaker minds...and I was absolutely one of those.*

Life lesson #20... *Make sure you're not getting hustled by a smarter person than you.*

Life lesson #21... *Be careful what you wish for...you might not like it when you get it.*

Life lesson #22... *I promise you; you can do whatever it is that you want to do if you want it bad enough. When your body says stop, you need your mind to be strong enough to override the pain and keep going. Train your mind to overcome your body.*

Life lesson #23... *Come on, man! Suck it up... Shots aren't that bad.*

Life lesson #24... *Sometimes what you are currently doing is a stepping stone to the next level. You're not going to start at the top. You need to learn first. Some of us need to learn more than others. Don't waste time complaining that what you're doing isn't helping you. The truth is you are probably learning more than you realize, and you probably need all the help you can get! Enjoy the journey. This is not the last thing you will do. It's just a chapter in your book.*

Life lesson #25... *You do not have to accept an answer that someone else gives you. They are not always right. In general, people do not expect you to challenge them. But if you think you're right, then you should absolutely challenge any answer you don't accept. You do not have to accept NO. You have options.*

Life lesson #26... *This is another big one...and sometimes hard to handle. The world is what it is. You will have to follow the rules if you want to succeed. You will have to absolutely jump through hoops that you don't want to.. You can scream about it, cry about it, fight it, and hate it, and it won't change a thing. At some point, you will learn to accept it and play the game within the rules, or you will end your life here on planet earth a failure. Life is not fair. Sometimes life is unjust. The world is not designed for you to succeed. You will have to fight for success. It's not easy. And you are not better prepared or smarter than everybody else. Nobody owes you anything. Achieving your goals will not happen quickly and, in fact, will probably take a long time, longer than you want it to take and longer than you thought it would take. The sooner you figure out what you need to do, the sooner you can begin the process of getting what you want in life. Some people figure that out early, some figure it out later, and some never figure it out and spend their life complaining about it.*

Life lesson #27... *I am less worried about where you are today and what you're doing than I am about your attitude and ambition. If you can figure out how to get those two factors right, your future is an open book. Where you start has absolutely nothing to do with where you can end up. That is up to you, and nobody else.*

Life lesson #28... *Make it a point to do all the things in life that have meaning. I was too angry to care about the little things, and today I regret it.*

Life lesson #29... *I had no idea what I was doing in business. I had no business even starting a business, but I did it anyway. I figured it out along the way. Building the airplane on the way down had been a theme of my life. I never knew what I was doing before; I just went out and did it. NEVER let your lack of experience, education, or training stop you from doing want you want to do, and NEVER listen to well-intentioned people who tell you that you can't do something!! Your future is in your hands, not theirs.*

Life lesson #30... *Be ready for the light bulb...and when it turns on; don't ignore it!*

Life lesson #31... *Do NOT live above your means. If you don't have the money to pay for what you want or the money in savings to back it up, don't buy it. The stress of being broke with a lot of possessions is not a good feeling. Don't do it.*

Life lesson #32... *Sometimes things need to fall apart so they can get better. Not every bad situation is actually bad. It may actually be really good, but you just can't see it yet. So don't get too excited when you think something bad has happened. Don't stress yourself out and cause unneeded problems. The better thing might be right around the corner.*

Life lesson #33...*You may have talents that you haven't discovered yet. These talents may lead you to bigger and better things. Don't be afraid to try something new, and don't be afraid of failing. You might find out you have an amazing future that you've never even thought about.*

Life lesson #34... *You can't keep on doing something that doesn't make you happy. Life is short. The older you get, the faster it moves. If you're not happy, change what makes you unhappy. Find a better way. Do something different. Don't be rash, about it but figure it out before it's too late.*

Life lesson #35... *Don't be greedy, and never underestimate the guy who's working for you. He might just be the next big thing. That guy who wouldn't give me the four points was out of the insurance business a couple of years later. I have no idea what happened to him, but he missed out on millions of dollars.*

Life lesson #36... *There will always be a better way to do something. Either you will figure it out or someone else will.*

Life lesson #37... *Yes, my whole world fell apart when the landscaping company crashed and burned. What I didn't know was that two and a half years later, I would be worth $1 million on paper. You have no idea what's around the next corner. So, just relax and wait for it. The truth is the only thing I'd lost was a landscaping company that made me unhappy every day. Once again, something that was bad at the moment became something much, much better. If my landscaping* *company had not failed so spectacularly, I would probably still be doing it and still be unhappy. That's a scary thought.*

Life lesson #38... *Protect your future. If you know what you're doing is the right thing, do not let somebody else talk you out of it. Do what you know is right.*

Life lesson #39... *When you work for someone else, your ideas and anything you create are not yours; they belong to the company you work for. You are just an employee, and all the whining and complaining and talk about how life isn't fair doesn't mean a thing. As long as you are working for somebody else, it is their ball and bat; it is their game. There's nothing you can do, so you need to get over it and move on.*

Life lesson #40... *If a pizza place closes, don't open another pizza place in the same spot. IT WON'T WORK!!!*

Life lesson #41... *If you have to finance something for somebody, chances are you're never going to get it. There is a reason they need you to finance it. It's usually because nobody else is dumb enough to give them financing. Second, if your business is failing, there's a pretty good chance the next guy is not going to be able to turn it around.*

Life lesson #42... *Money is not as important as loyalty. I could have made the easy decision to take money in one deal in particular and sever a relationship, but I made the decision to be loyal. If I had betrayed him, I would have been out of business in a year. By remaining true, I made over $10 million in three years.*

Life lesson #43... *Sometimes you need to take the risk. Sometimes you need to bet on other people and not just yourself. Follow the track record.*

Life lesson #44... *Stress is a killer. I mean it. Stress can actually kill you. It destroys your body slowly over time, and you don't even know it's happening. If you are stressed, you need to figure out how to make it go away. This is critical. You need to figure it out now and not later. Once it tears you apart, it's too late to fix it.*

Life lesson #45... *Understand what is most important in your life. Your family means more than anything—it especially outranks money. Money is awesome and can provide a wonderful life if used properly, but it is not everything.*

I heard a saying that fits here: "I've been poor, and I've been rich, and I will take rich every time..." But it's not worth trading your family for. You can have both, but you have to be happy along the way, or it will not be worth it in the end.

Life lesson #46... *If you have access to someone to help guide you in life and if you have someone who loves you and is there for you to get advice from, use them. Life is so much easier when you have people helping you not to make mistakes.*

Life lesson #47... *If you're about to hit rock bottom, make sure you put yourself in the presence of someone who is willing, qualified, and can help you. You are in a state of weakness, and you do not want the wrong information or advice getting into your mind while you start* *building <u>new healthy</u> walls. Because once the new information or new beliefs are in there, behind those new walls, <u>they are</u> not leaving unless you hit rock bottom again. The change that you need to make will depend on the people and information you put in your mind. Be very selective of what you allow to be in your mind behind those walls.*

Life lesson #48... *People can change. I know you hear all the time that people can't, but they can. It might take a devastating event in their life, or they might have to hit rock bottom, but believe me, they can change.*

Life lesson #49... *Be nice to strangers... They might be your brother or sister!!!*

Life lesson #50... Lying to your children is never a good idea. Lying to them about something so big only to have them find out decades later is even worse. Just tell them the truth. They will respect you more and get over it more easily than if they have been subject to a lifetime of lies and deceit.

Life lesson #51... *Never buy something without doing your due diligence. Just because somebody is giving you a price doesn't mean they won't take less...sometimes a LOT less.*

Life lesson #52... *If your first offer doesn't insult them, you offered too much. Remember, I offered zero dollars to Bob, and that I saved myself $50,000-100,000. Business is brutal... ALWAYS lowball... Always, as you have nothing to lose.*

Life lesson #53... *Success in one area does not make you a genius in other areas.*

Life lesson #54... *Do your homework. Understand ALL the variables before you sign a deal. Do not feel bad about making the best deal for you. Nobody else is looking out for you. You have to look out for yourself and your family.*

Life Lesson #55... *Sometimes you win, and sometimes you learn.*

Life lesson #56... *Let it go. If it comes back to you, it was yours. If it doesn't, it never was.*

Life lesson #57... *Sometimes it takes years to accomplish a goal. Don't be discouraged if your goals don't come fast or easy. Don't drop them just because you didn't get them done when you wanted to. I sat on this half-finished book for five years. Now, it's done. I get to check off writing my book from the list, and that is exciting for me!*

ACKNOWLEDGMENTS

As I thought about who to acknowledge in this book, my mind wandered around to all the people I talk about in here and how they've affected my life and helped to get me where I am today.

Where would I be if my junior high band director hadn't spent time with me and encouraged me to be a better musician?

Would I have graduated high school if the daughter of the school secretary hadn't had a crush on me and her mom hadn't forgotten to report my absences from school?

If the school counselor had just taken me to the principal's office that day, instead of to the Air Force recruiter's speech, I would never have gone into the military.

What about my senior year high school English teacher who allowed me to write my final paper for her class on the *Tarzan* book series instead of whatever classic novel everyone else had to read. She could have just failed me in the class, but instead allowed me to pass and graduate.

Where would I be without the guy I met working at the pizza place when I was eighteen, and who recruited me into the Amway business? I never made any money, but he exposed me to so many positive people who told me I could do whatever I wanted to do in life. I made more money from those lessons than anything I ever learned in school.

I can't even imagine where I would be if my friend in the insurance business hadn't tried so hard over so many months to get me to come sell insurance with him. He started my life on a path that led to millions of dollars of income and so many business opportunities I would never have come across.

Then there is my friend and mentor who I stayed loyal to when his life hit a tough spot. He re-launched a business with me a year later, and three years after that, we sold our biggest company together, which set us up for life financially. I will always be grateful to him for teaching me to be a better businessman and human being.

Finally, my ex-wife and kids... She for supporting me through all the crazy years of being broke and desperate...and my kids just for being awesome.

Thank you to all of these people and more...who shaped my life.

ABOUT THE AUTHOR

Brian Will is a serial entrepreneur who launched five very successful companies in four different industries over the last thirty-five years. His first foray into owning his own business was a 10-year stint in the landscaping industry that he started when he was twenty years old. This was followed by three online internet companies during the dot com boom of the late nineties and early 2000s.

The first was an online health insurance website and call center that was eventually sold to a venture capital company in Silicon Valley and today is one of the largest online Medicare insurance platforms in the US.

The second was an online "lead generation" company in the subprime credit space that was sold to a private equity firm out of Chicago.

The third was another online health insurance website and call center that was sold to another venture capital company in Silicon Valley and today is one of the largest individual state health insurance exchange platforms.

These four exits were followed by several years of consulting projects for both private and public companies in the field of sales and management training.

Although he tried to quit working on multiple occasions, it just wasn't in his nature to sit back and do nothing.

Today Brian owns a growing chain of restaurants in the Atlanta area while he splits his time between the suburbs of Atlanta, Georgia, and Clearwater Beach, Florida.

He is also the very proud father of two adult children.

Having traveled to 25+ countries around the world, Brian considers himself a world-traveler, adventure seeker, and adrenaline junkie, but will always be a sucker for a McDonald's coke and some fries.